133 T

MARVELS & MYSTERIES
GHOSTS

PARRAGON

CONTENTS

INTRODUCTION

Grey-habited nuns walking through stone walls; headless wraiths stalking long, panelled corridors; insubstantial coaches barrelling through the night; old, disused rooms whose very fabric seems to be suffused with a chill, hair-pricking dread; mysterious moans, phantom foot-falls and the clanking of chains: all these have become clichés of the horror story over the past two centuries, but all of them, too, have been witnessed and reported by apparently sane and sober witnesses.

This book examines some of the evidence for the existence of ghosts and the theories advanced to explain them. Are they the souls of the unquiet dead, doomed to roam the earth because the way to the afterlife is somehow blocked, or do ghostly manifestations have some other cause? Can places somehow record impressions of great emotion, which sensitive people can 'read' centuries later? Do mischievous spirits hammer on walls or tables and send heavy objects spinning through the air, or is it the untrammelled sexual energy of an adolescent that causes such poltergeist phenomena? Are some people or places cursed? And where do those other fabled denizens of the dark night, vampires and werewolves, fit into all this?

The book also takes another look at some famous and not so famous hauntings. The tale of Borley Rectory, once dubbed 'the most haunted house in Britain' is told in some detail, and so is the story of its less celebrated, but perhaps more genuinely ghostly, church. There are several stories from Scotland, whose bloody history and legacy of sombre, stone buildings has made it strangely susceptible to ghostly tales, while the USA provides the story of the murderous poltergeist known as the 'Bell Witch'.

THE BELL WITCH STRIKES

THE MOST SAVAGE AND RELENTLESS POLTERGEIST ON RECORD MUST SURELY BE THE 'BELL WITCH', WHOSE SYSTEMATIC PERSECUTION OF THE BELL FAMILY OF TENNESSEE, USA, IN THE EARLY 19TH CENTURY, STOPPED ONLY AT MURDER

In the illustration below, slaves on a cotton plantation – similar to the one owned by the Bell family – practise a voodoo ceremony. The Bells may have been influenced by such an atmosphere of belief in the paranormal.

It has become almost axiomatic that ghosts do no physical harm to those who experience them. Indeed, apparitions are frequently reported as being solid and 'normal'; and it is only when they walk away through the wall or disappear as if 'switched off' that the observer realises what he has seen and becomes alarmed. Even the rumbustious poltergeist – whose activities include such apparently dangerous acts as throwing stones, smashing glass and crockery, and starting fires – causes little or no bodily damage to its victims.

But there is one well-attested case of a supernatural power, which not only seems to have killed its victim but apparently set out to do so with deliberate intent – the so-called 'Bell Witch'. The late Dr Nandor Fodor, a Freudian psychiatrist and pioneer of modern psychophysical research, called the case 'America's greatest ghost story'; but if his conclusions are correct, it must also rank as one of the world's most bizarre murder mysteries.

The malevolent power that laid siege to the homestead of John Bell and his family in Robertson County, Tennessee, USA, during the year 1817 lay totally outside the experience of that rural but rich community. A century and a quarter had elapsed since America's only serious outbreak of witchcraft mania died down at Salem, Massachusetts; while the Fox sisters of Hydesville, New York, founding daughters of modern Spiritualism, lay more than 30 years in the future. The term 'poltergeist' was in fact unknown at the time.

The Bells and their neighbours were Bible-belt Christians with a streak of superstition that paralleled that of their slaves: both black and white consulted a village 'wise woman' named Kate Batt. It was natural that they should call their trouble by an old name. As Dr Fodor put it:

'The "Witch", as the haunter was called, serves well as a descriptive term... modern poltergeists, no matter how much mischief and destruction they wreak, stop short of murder. The Bell Witch did not, and it only ceased its activities after the death by poisoning of John Bell, the head of the household,

The Puritans, above, are seen arresting a 'witch' during the infamous outbreak of witchcraft mania at Salem, Massachusetts, in 1692, when 30 people were accused of sorcery and 19 of them hanged. Although most American rural areas, like those in Europe, had their 'wise women' and natural psychics, from the end of the Salem trials to 1817, when the Bell Witch first made itself known, paranormality in the United States had not been a burning issue. But then – literally, as far as the Bell family was concerned – all hell broke loose.

youth been at the centre of the phenomena – and perhaps even an unwitting murderer.

John Bell was a prosperous cotton plantation owner, well-liked and respected by his neighbours and friends, among them General Andrew Jackson, who was to become seventh President of the United States and a witness to the Witch's activities. John and his wife, Luce, lived in a large, two-storey house with their nine children. Their domestic servants and plantation hands were black slaves; but – as far as was possible under such conditions – the Bell children mingled with the hands on terms of easy familiarity and friendliness. One of the most outgoing was Betsy Bell, a robust and apparently contented 12-year-old.

DISTURBING THE PEACE

The manifestations began in the form of knocks and raps on the walls and windows of the house. These increased in power and volume so that, by the end of the year, they were literally shaking the building to its foundations. Gnawing, scratching and flapping sounds alternated with the rattle of invisible stones on the roof, the clattering of what sounded like heavy chains on the floor, and half-human gulping, choking and 'lip smacking' noises.

Then, one day, the force displayed its strength, pulling Richard Bell's hair so violently that it lifted him clear of his bed. He felt 'that the top of his head had been taken off .... Immediately, Joel yelled out in great fright, and next Elizabeth was screaming in her room, and after that something was continually pulling at her hair after she retired to bed.'

Up to this point, the family had kept their curious troubles to themselves, but now they let a close friend and neighbour, James Johnson, into their secret. After witnessing the phenomena for himself, Johnson concluded that some intelligence lay behind them. He performed a brief exorcism, and this did seem to silence the Bell house for a while.

But the Witch returned – and with renewed vigour, slapping Betsy's cheeks until they were crimson and pulling her hair until she screamed with pain.

John Bell and James Johnson now called in more neighbours to form an investigating committee, partly to keep the tormented Betsy company, and partly to induce the Witch to speak.

Betsy spent a night away from home; but the 'trouble followed her with the same severity, disturbing the family where she went as it did at home, nor were we any wise relieved', according to a later account given by Richard Bell. Indeed, the committee itself seems to have done more harm than good. In fact, the development of the Witch's voice seems to have come about under the urgings of the committee. At first, it was low and inarticulate – a thin, whistling sound – but gradually it turned into a weak faltering whisper and, towards the end of its career, it became loud and raucous. Unlike the other physical phenomena, which took place only after dark – although usually in lamplit rooms – the voice could be heard both day and night, and came from any direction. And as the voice grew in strength, so did the Witch's violence.

'The blows were heard distinctly, like the open palm of a heavy hand, while the sting was keenly

whom it tortured and persecuted with a fury of unrelenting savagery.'

The phenomena began in 1817 and petered out in the late spring of 1821, some months after the death of John Bell, although they did reoccur briefly seven years later, apparently to fulfil a promise to one of the dead man's sons. During its reign, the Witch also attracted hordes of ghost hunters, most of them anxious to prove it a hoax. But these all met, according to contemporary records, with 'egregious defeat'.

Richard Williams Bell, a younger son of the family, wrote an account of the phenomena, entitled *Our Family Trouble*, in 1846, when he was 36 years old; and although he was only 10 when the Witch ceased its activity, his account tied in with later, more detailed records. One of these, published in 1867 by a Clarksville newspaper editor, M.V. Ingram, included interviews with all surviving members of the family and contemporary witnesses, as well as the testimony of the author, who had himself witnessed the outbreak as a child. Another was a document by John Bell Jr, as related to his son, Dr Joel Thomas Bell. The definitive version was given in 1934 by Dr Charles Bailey Bell, son of Dr Joel, who lectured on neurosurgery at the University of Nashville's Medical Department, was a consultant at Nashville City Hospital, and a prominent member of several national medical bodies. As a young medical student in 1888, Dr Charles Bell had interviewed his great aunt Elizabeth 'Betsy' Bell about her recollections: then 83, she had in her felt,' we are told; and they were rained indiscriminately on anyone who happened to be around, but particularly on Betsy Bell and her father, John.

From the beginning, the force had seemed to centre on Betsy; and as the voice developed, so the formerly robust girl began to suffer fainting fits and breathing difficulties that lasted up to half-an-hour at a time. During these attacks, the Witch remained silent; but as soon as Betsy had recovered, it would begin to talk again. The obvious conclusion was that, somehow, Betsy was producing sounds by ventriloquism; but a doctor who visited the house laid his hands over her mouth at the time the voice was heard, and soon satisfied himself that she was in no way connected with these noises.

VOICED OBSCENITIES

When the voice first developed, its utterances tended to be of a pious nature. It could reproduce, word for word, for instance, the Sunday sermons of the two local parsons, imitating their tones exactly. It sang beautifully, and recited tracts from *The Bible*. Unfortunately, however, this was only a temporary phase. The voice soon began uttering obscenities, which were particularly distressing to a Bible-belt family. It also alarmed them by claiming to be 'Old Kate Batt's witch'.

The Witch's ability to produce disgusting odours was also demonstrated on several occasions, once to local witness William Porter when the Witch got into bed with him and twisted his bedclothes off him 'just like a boy would roll himself in a quilt'. Porter leaped out of bed and picked up the roll of bedclothes, intending to throw them into the fire. He said: 'I discovered it was very weighty and smelled awful. I had not got halfway across the room before the luggage got so heavy and became so offensive that I was compelled to drop it on the floor and rush out of doors for a breath of fresh air. The odour... was the most offensive stench I ever smelled... absolutely stifling.'

Once Porter had recovered, however, he came back into the room and shook out the bedclothes, only to find the mysterious extra weight had vanished – and that the stink had evaporated.

Like many other poltergeists, the Witch also produced apports. During Luce Bell's Bible study meetings, it took to dropping fresh fruit, as if from nowhere, on to the table or into the laps of those present; and once, on Betsy's birthday, it produced a large basket of oranges, bananas, grapes and nuts, claiming: 'These came from the West Indies. I brought them myself.'

But perhaps more in keeping with the Witch's real nature was the scatological prank it played on Betsy Bell, when a local quack doctor offered her a potion to rid her of the power that tormented her. It was an unpleasant mixture, and the quack warned her that it would make her very ill. A copious evacuation of the stomach followed, the Witch roaring with laughter at the surprise of the household when Betsy's vomit and excrement were found to be full of pins and needles. Richard Bell wrote:

They were real brass pins and needles. Mother kept them as long as she lived. I have seen the pins and needles myself. As a matter of course, Betsy could not have lived with such a conglomeration in her stomach, and the only solution to the matter

*In*FOCUS

WITCH ON THE WAGON

When Andrew Jackson (1767-1845), seventh president of the United States, was a general in the army he took a wagon, pulled by a team of army horses, to visit his old friend John Bell. To his horror and surprise, he was treated to a startling demonstration of the Bell Witch's superhuman physical strength.

As Jackson drove up to the house, the wagon suddenly ground to a halt, despite the enormous efforts of the driver and horses, straining at the traces. Unable to find any natural cause for the stoppage, the general cried: 'By the eternal boys! It is the Witch!'

At this point, a sharp, metallic voice – apparently coming from the nearby bushes – said: 'All right, general, let the wagon move.' And the wagon started to roll forward once again, towards the house. The Bell Witch, it seemed, had wanted to prove its abilities to the visitors.

was that the Witch dropped the pins and needles in the excrement unobserved.'

As time went on, the Witch ceased its physical attacks on Betsy, but began instead to torment her emotionally. She had become engaged in her early teens to a local man, Joshua Gardner, to whom, apparently, everyone in the family and neighbourhood thought she was ideally suited. But from the moment it developed the power of speech, the Witch derided Joshua and advised against the match whispering: 'Please Betsy Bell, don't have Joshua Gardner, please Betsy Bell, don't marry Joshua Gardner.' Eventually, it grew sharper in its remonstrations, making embarrassing revelations

The statue, below, is of a Roman house god, or family guardian, known as the lar familiaris. Although in many Roman households, religion was treated as a mere formality, the household gods were often genuinely revered. Indeed, keeping evil out of one's home and family circle has always preoccupied Mankind, and the Bell family fell foul of this omnipresent threat. Even in our so-called 'progressive' society, exorcists are kept busy ejecting 'evil forces' from family homes.

Hollywood's expression of paranormal violence is depicted in a scene from the film The Omen, *above. The disruption occasioned by real-life poltergeists is often more psychological than physical, but the Bell Witch attacked its victims on all fronts – socially, psychologically and physically.*

about the young couple's relationship in front of friends, and promising that Betsy would never know a moment's peace if she married Joshua. Eventually, hysterical and in despair, she returned his engagement ring.

THREATS MADE GOOD

But behind all these developments lay the Witch's implacable hatred for John Bell, head of the family. From the start, the Witch had sworn that it would torment Old Jack Bell to the end of his life – and it made good its threat.

On 19 December 1820, John Bell was discovered in his bed in a deep stupor and could not be roused. His son, John, went to the medicine cabinet; but instead of the prescribed medicine, he found 'a smokey looking vial, which was about one-third full of dark-coloured liquid'.

The doctor arrived in time to hear the Witch crowing: 'It's useless for you to try and relieve Old Jack – I have got him this time; he will never get up from that bed again.' Asked about the strange medicine, it said: 'I put it there, and gave Old Jack a big dose out of it last night while he was fast asleep, which fixed him.'

Neither the doctor, nor any member of the household, could explain the presence of the mystery bottle, but a rather arbitrary test was made of its contents: the doctor dunked a straw into the mixture and wiped it on to the tongue of the Bells' pet cat. 'The cat jumped and whirled over a few times, stretched out, kicked, and died very quickly,' according to a contemporary account.

The doctor's next action would be unforgivable today, and even in his own time would have drawn suspicion had he done it in Europe; but his scientific

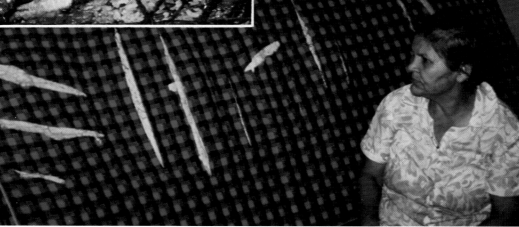

Witch vanished for good, pausing only to say that it would return again in 'one hundred years and seven' to a descendant. As Dr Fodor remarked, this doubtful honour should have fallen to Dr Charles Bailey Bell; but the year of 1935 came and went, and the Bell Witch failed to keep its tryst.

So what actually occurred on the Bell plantation? Even allowing for distortion of some of the details with the passage of time, it seems that the principal events did take place. In 1849, the *Saturday Evening Post* investigated the case, and printed an article alleging that 12-year-old Betsy had engineered the whole thing. The Bell family lawyers obtained a substantial amount in damages, and the magazine printed a retraction. The hoax theory, then, seems patently absurd.

training seems to have been overcast by the superstition of rural 19th-century Tennessee. He threw the bottle into the fire, thereby disposing of the Witch's brew for good.

The following morning, John Bell was found dead in his bed; and the Witch marked his passing – whether or not this was by its hand – by singing ribald songs at his funeral.

Dissipated Energy
After the death of John Bell, the energy of the Witch seemed to dissipate until, at last, having achieved its ends, the Witch seemed content to go. The final phenomenon, which to Dr Fodor was 'highly symbolic of guilt release', took place some years later. Something like a cannonball rolled down the chimney and burst in a puff of smoke, and a clear voice called out: 'I'm going, and will be gone for seven years.'

This promise was fulfilled, for seven years later the Witch did indeed return. At the time, Mrs Bell and her sons, Richard and Joel, were the only occupants of the homestead, Betsy having married another man.

Scratching sounds were heard, and half-hearted pulling of bedclothes felt. The family agreed to ignore the manifestations; and after a fortnight, the

Brazil, a country much preoccupied by Spiritism, also suffers from frequent and sometimes severe outbreaks of paranormal vandalism. In one case, a pet parrot fell victim to a poltergeist's spite and had its tail feathers singed, as shown top; *and in another, a group of people discovered that the settee on which they were sitting was being slashed by an invisible assailant, as* above. *But few people have suffered anything as extreme as the indignities and horrors of the Bell family.*

As Dr Fodor pointed out, Betsy's fainting and dizzy spells – immediately followed by the voice of the Witch – seem very similar to the symptoms exhibited by a medium going into a trance. On the other hand, the Witch, although describing itself as 'a spirit from everywhere' on one occasion, denied all knowledge of life after death.

Dr Fodor concluded that Betsy Bell suffered from a split personality, and that in some mysterious way, part of her subconscious mind had taken on a life of its own, literally plaguing her father to death. The psychology of such splits is still a mystery, and similar cases are rare – but when they do occur, some powerful emotional shock is usually found to have been the triggering factor. Dr Fodor also made the purely speculative guess that John Bell had interfered with his daughter sexually during her early childhood, and that the onset of puberty and her awakening sexuality stirred the long suppressed memory of that interference – bringing into being the Bell Witch.

But Fodor admitted that no conventional psychologist would credit split personalities with manifestations and powers outside the range of the body. As he concluded: 'Obviously we are dealing with facts for which we have no adequate theories within normal or abnormal psychology.'

UNDERSTANDING GHOSTS

**TROUBLED SPIRITS OF THE DEAD AND PHANTOM
ANIMALS HAVE BOTH APPEARED AS GHOSTS. BUT
ARE THEY, IN ESSENCE, THE SAME? WHAT DO
VARIOUS TYPES OF HAUNTING HAVE IN COMMON?**

The perennial question as to whether ghosts exist must, in view of various surveys carried out by societies for psychical research over the last 100 years or so, be answered in the affirmative – if only because to reject the testimony of the many hundreds of respectable people who claim to have experienced apparitions as wishful thinking, self-delusion or downright lying would clearly be sheer wilfulness.

The question now facing parapsychologists and researchers into the paranormal is: *how* do ghosts exist? Are they revenant spirits? Are they the result of telepathy? Or are they produced by mass hallucination or self-hypnosis? Advances in psychology over the last few decades have brought us nearer to understanding some aspects of apparitions, but the definitive truth still eludes us.

The most common form of 'ghost' appears to be the 'crisis apparition', which occurs when a person under great stress – sometimes on the point of death – appears to someone close, like a blood relation, as a 'vision' or, occasionally, as a disembodied voice. Indeed, the majority of crisis apparition cases have tragic overtones. For instance, soldiers have appeared to mothers or wives at the exact time of their own deaths on faraway battlefields. But not all apparitions are associated with unhappy events.

Victoria Branden, in her book *Understanding Ghosts*, quotes the case of a friend who was

The photograph, below, of the library at Combermere Abbey in Cheshire was taken on 5 December 1891 by Sybell Corbet, who had been staying at the house. When she developed the plate, she was startled to see the shape of an elderly gentleman sitting in a chair on the left of the picture. The figure was later identified as that of Lord Combermere himself: but at the time the photograph was taken, he was actually being buried a few miles away.

evacuated from England to Canada during the Second World War because of a health problem, leaving her husband behind in the Services. One evening, the children were busy with their homework, while their mother was ironing in what she admitted to Victoria Branden was 'a rather dreamlike state'.

Suddenly, she saw the door of the room open, and her uniformed husband came in. But before she could recover from her astonishment, he vanished. She put down the iron and sat, near to fainting, in a chair. The children clustered around her anxiously; and when she told them what had happened, they said that they had not seen anything and the door certainly had not opened. The mother and the elder child had, however, read of crisis apparitions and became convinced that the vision meant that the husband had been killed or injured. They made a note of the time and circumstances, but agonisingly, that was all they could do.

Some days later, to what must have been their enormous relief, news came: the husband had been unexpectedly chosen to go on a training programme to Canada, and was to be stationed at a camp very near to his family. This meant, of course, that he could live with them while abroad. When the couple were finally reunited, the husband said that the news had come as a happy shock. He could not remember consciously 'projecting' any thought to his wife, but they worked out that he had probably opened his commanding officer's door after hearing the news at the moment when his wife had 'seen' her door open and the vision of her husband enter.

An interesting point about this incident is that the wife was 'rather dreamlike' at the time, with her mind in an open and receptive state. Meanwhile, the children, who saw nothing, were concentrating hard on their homework.

Exactly how such information is communicated remains a mystery, particularly in the case where an apparition appears solid and living. However, scientists point out that perception is a much more complex business than at first appears: vivid dreams, for instance, often appear perfectly solid and physical, and in such cases the percipient is certainly not receiving information through his eyes. A hypnotist may tell a subject that, when he or she awakes, only the hypnotist will be in the room – even though other people may be present. Then, when the subject comes around, he will not see the others present until the hypnotist removes the suggestion. Something like this may also occur in cases of crisis apparition, although it seems remarkable that the agent – or person 'sending' the hallucination – can achieve at a distance, and in many cases while he is unconscious, what the hypnotist can only manage by giving specific instructions.

Evidence actually points to the fact that the agent's mind plays a smaller part in crisis apparitions than does that of the percipient. If we look at recorded cases, it becomes apparent that the agent rarely appears as he is at the moment of 'transmission' – the percipient does not see a mangled body in a motor car, or a dying wounded soldier in a trench, but what appears to be a normal image of the agent that, moreover, relates to the percipient's surroundings.

This point is stressed by G. N. M. Tyrrell in his book *Apparitions*. He points out that apparitions in crisis cases have even been guilty of such unghostlike phenomena as casting shadows or appearing reflected in a mirror. As he put it:

'[They] adapt themselves almost miraculously to the physical conditions of the percipient's surroundings, of which the agent as a rule can know little or nothing. These facts reveal the apparition to be a piece of stage machinery which the percipient must have a large hand in creating and some of the details for which he must supply – that is to say, an apparition cannot be merely a direct expression of the agent's idea; it must be a drama worked out with that idea as its motif.'

But telepathy can only partly explain cases of collective apparitions, where a group of people witness the same thing. What is more, by definition, the telepathic agent must be a sentient being; so it

Cases of crisis apparitions are most common in times of war, when a mother may see her son at the moment of his death on a battlefield, as below. It seems that the shock of death causes some kind of telepathic communication between son and mother. But rarely does the mother have a vision of a dying soldier; in most cases, she sees her son as he appeared in normal, everyday life.

is hard to see how any concrete object appearing as an apparition can do so as a result of telepathy. One of the most famous cases of a collective apparition was reported to the Society for Psychical Research in the late 19th century by Charles Lett, the son-in-law of a certain Captain Towns. One day at about 9 p.m., some six weeks after the Captain's death, his daughter, Mrs Lett, and a Miss Berthon entered a bedroom at his home. The gas light was burning:

'And they were amazed to see, reflected in the polished surface of the wardrobe, the image of Captain Towns. It was . . . like an ordinary medallion portrait, but life-size. The face appeared wan and pale . . . and he wore a kind of grey flannel jacket, in which he had been accustomed to sleep. Surprised and half alarmed at what they saw, their first idea was that a portrait had been hung in the room and that what they saw was its reflection – but there was no picture of the kind. Whilst they were looking and wondering, my wife's sister, Miss Towns, came into the room; and before any of the others

When apparitions not seen at the time – such as that shown left – turn up on photographic prints, some believe it may be due to the film being more sensitive to surroundings than the photographer. When the photographer sees something that the camera fails to capture, however, it may be because of human hypersensitivity.

❝ DO NOT LET US FEAR THE DEAD WHEN THEY COME TO US, BUT DO NOT LET US ALLOW A PANIC-STRICKEN DISEMBODIED ENTITY TO CLUTCH US ROUND THE NECK LIKE A DROWNING MAN, IN ITS EFFORTS TO REMAIN ON THE PLANE OF FORM... TO DO SO IS NOT TO HELP HIM, BUT TO CONDEMN HIM TO A TERRIBLE FATE, THE FATE OF THE EARTH-BOUND. ❞

DION FORTUNE, THROUGH THE GATES OF DEATH

had time to speak, she exclaimed: "Good gracious! Do you see Papa?"

'One of the housemaids passing by was called into the room. Immediately she cried:"Oh miss! The Master!" The captain's own servant, the butler, and the nurse were also called in and immediately recognised him. Finally, Mrs Towns was sent for and, seeing the apparition, advanced towards it with her arm extended as if to touch it. As she passed her hand over the panel of the wardrobe, the figure gradually faded away and never again appeared.'

Those parapsychologists who lean towards a telepathic origin for all apparitions would probably say that the vision was seen first by either Mrs Letts or Miss Berthon, who then passed it on by thought transference to each arrival. But where did the vision come from in the first place?

An early pioneer of psychical research, F. W. H. Myers, author of *Human Personality and its Survival of Bodily Death,* suggested that it was the revenant spirit or 'essence' of Captain Towns, taking a last look at his old home six weeks after death. Myers said that an apparition 'may be a manifestation of

THE GHOST THAT GREW AND GREW

One of the main problems facing the objective psychical researcher is that of sheer human gullibility. People like a good ghost story and tend to embellish any narrative – so that after a few retellings, the stark facts soon become wrapped up in a cocoon of invention.

In the summer of 1970, Frank Smyth, who was at that time an associate editor of the magazine *Man, Myth and Magic,* set out to examine the form taken by such gullibility. He therefore invented a ghost, complete with location, background and 'witnesses', and published the story in the magazine.

The invention was completely random. One Sunday morning, Smyth had gone down to London's Docklands to meet John Philby, son of super-spy 'Kim' Philby. Philby's building company was renovating a site at Ratcliffe Wharf, and Smyth decided that the deserted dock was sufficiently eerie to provide a location for his ghost. Hard by Ratcliffe Wharf was the semi-derelict church of St Anne; and this, plus the fact that it was a Sunday morning, influenced Smyth into making his 'ghost' that of a clergyman. Alongside the wharf runs Ratcliffe Highway, once – at least until the late 19th century – a thoroughfare of brothels, grog shops, and cheap boarding houses. The proximity of this old road suggested to Smyth that his vicar had been the owner of a sailors' rooming house, and that he had robbed 'homeward-bounders' (seamen newly paid off from ships in the Thames), had killed them in their lodgings, and disposed of their bodies in the river. Thus the background for the imaginary ghost was swiftly set up.

Philby, himself a former war correspondent, and Smyth then decided that witnesses were important. Together with one of Philby's employees, they lent their names to the fiction that they had seen the ghost – the figure of an old white-haired man with a walking stick. They also agreed that if anyone, either researcher or interested enquirer, asked about the 'phenomenon', they would immediately confess that it was invented.

Frank Smyth, inventor of the ghost of Ratcliffe Wharf, is seen below, in front of the church of *St Anne.*

CASEBOOK

Smyth then wrote up the story as a 'factual' article in *Man, Myth and Magic.* No one ever queried the credentials of the 'Phantom Vicar of Ratcliffe Wharf'; but over the next twelve months or so, eight books purporting to tell the stories of genuine ghosts appeared, each featuring the phantom vicar. Only one, by a London *Sunday Times* feature writer, treated the subject with some scepticism: the others not only recounted the tale without critical comment, but one, by a well-known writer on the supernatural, actually embellished it to a marked degree.

In 1973, Smyth wrote an article for the *Sunday Times,* telling of his experiment and subsequently appeared in a BBC2 film entitled *A Leap in the Dark.* This film, too, told the story of the invention, but it also featured a number of people who claimed actually to have seen the phantom vicar. One man said that he had witnessed an old man in 18th-century clerical garb walking in the roadway outside the 'Town of Ramsgate' pub, near St Katherine's Dock – a good half-mile from Ratcliffe Wharf. The writer Jilly Cooper told of interviewing a police superintendent who, on retirement from the River Branch of the Metropolitan force, had said that, as a young man, he had been unwilling to enter Ratcliffe Wharf for fear of the ghostly priest. And a Thames waterman claimed that he had seen the shadowy form of the vicar standing on Ratcliffe Wharf some months before the story appeared in the magazine. After the television programme, many other letters were sent to the BBC, most of them apparently sincere, telling of further sightings.

There is absolutely no foundation for the Ratcliffe Wharf story. Nowhere in the records of Wapping – nor indeed any other part of London's Docklands – does there feature any tale of a ghostly cleric. The fact is that apparently rational people still claim to see the apparition in the area – despite its widespread refutation. One psychical researcher, however, has since suggested that Smyth's ghost may well have existed after all, and that it somehow made itself known to him via what only seems to have been imagination.

persistent personal energy' and quoted several cases to illustrate his point.

In one, a travelling salesman arrived at a hotel in Boston, Massachusetts, and sat working in his room when he suddenly became aware of a presence and looked up to see his sister, who had died nine years previously. As he sprang delightedly to his feet and called her name, she vanished, and yet he had time to take in every detail. 'She appeared as if alive,' he said, but added that there was a small red scratch on her right cheek.

Disturbed, he made an unscheduled stop at his parents' home and told them of his experience. When he mentioned the scratch, his mother was overcome with emotion, and explained that she had made the scratch on the dead body of her daughter accidentally, as she was preparing her for burial. Two weeks later, the mother died.

Myers wrote that the figure was 'not the corpse with the dull mark on which the mother's regretful thoughts might dwell, but . . . the girl in health and happiness, with the symbolic red mark worn simply as a test of identity.' He also suggested that the

Unfortunately, unlike the ghosts of well-rounded fiction, these 'haunting' apparitions do not seem to make much sense in their actions: they carry on in a mundane fashion, either wandering about or simply staring out of windows.

By and large, parapsychologists tend to theorise that, in certain cases, a kind of psychic record may be imprinted on a location, perhaps because of some violence or strong emotion generated there. In these cases, the apparition would not be a sentient spirit, but merely a projection like a cinema film. This certainly seems to be a likely explanation. It also ties in with the telepathy theories: for, if a person can send an image of himself telepathically to a percipient, may he not also be able to send a sort of 'free floating' image that hangs, as it were, in the atmosphere to be picked up by anyone sensitive enough to receive it?

Such a concept would also explain the occasionally convincing 'photographs' of apparitions: in such cases, the photographic film may be more sensitive to the surroundings than its operator; conversely, where a photographer sees a ghost but his camera

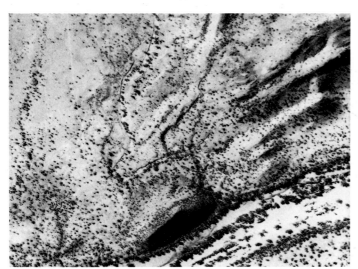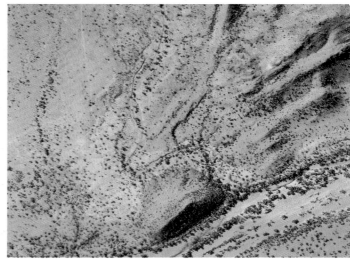

apparition was the spirit of the dead girl inducing her brother to go home and see their mother before she died.

Where an apparition persistently 'haunts' a place or a house – or sometimes even a person – believers in an afterlife assert that the spirit is trapped in its earthly environment, perhaps because of some unfulfilled task, or for the purpose of punishment.

❚❚ IT IS POSSIBLE THAT SOME PEOPLE ARE ENDOWED WITH A PARTICULAR GHOST-SEEING FACULTY... AND THAT THE APPARITION IS VISIBLE ONLY... TO THOSE WHO ARE EQUIPPED WITH THE APPROPRIATE RECEIVER. ❚❚

HILARY EVANS,

GODS: SPIRITS: COSMIC GUARDIANS

Ghost photographs often show images unseen by the human eye, as film is inherently more sensitive to certain light frequencies. The difference is rather like that between a picture shot with a standard film, above left, and one taken with infra-red equipment, above right. The infra-red photograph shows a tract of Australian desert more clearly and with much sharper detail, and provides information not otherwise available.

fails to do so, with nothing showing up in the prints, it may be *he* who is hypersensitive.

If such phantom recordings are indeed possible, it may also be that they are not necessarily fixed for ever. Andrew Green, in his book *Ghost Hunting*, quotes an interesting case of a woman in a red shoes, a red dress and a black head-dress, reported to haunt a mansion in 18th-century England. In the early 19th century, it was reported that the apparition was that of a lady in pink shoes, a pink dress, and a grey head-dress. She was not witnessed again until the mid-19th century, by which time the figure had dwindled to 'a lady in a white gown and with grey hair'. Just before the Second World War, all that was reported was 'the sound of a woman walking along the corridor and the swish of her dress'. In 1971, shortly before the demolition of the property involved, workmen felt merely 'a presence in one of the old corridors'.

Modern scientific research – into, for instance, the baffling field of quantum physics – constantly produces new slants on old phenomena. Ghosts – whether human or non-human – may yet prove to belong to a sphere of reality so far undreamed of.

CELTIC HARBINGERS OF DEATH

THE WAILING OF THE BANSHEE TO HERALD DEATH IS A WELL-KNOWN PART OF IRISH FOLKLORE. RECENT CASES SEEM TO INDICATE THE MOURNER MAY STILL BE ALIVE TODAY

One night early in 1979, Irene McCormack of Andover, Hampshire, England, was lying in bed when she heard what she later described as 'the most awful wailing noise'. She was alone in the house at the time and was deeply depressed, for her mother was close to death in Winchester Hospital.

When she heard the wailing, she nearly fell out of bed. 'I got up, shaking, and went downstairs; the dog was running round and round the living room, whimpering.' He would not settle, so Mrs McCormack took him upstairs to the bedroom where, after the wailing had died away, they both lay waiting for daybreak.

With the dawn came a police message for Mrs McCormack: she was asked to go to the bedside of her mother. When she arrived at the hospital, she found her in a coma. Irene McCormack stayed with her mother until the old lady's death a short time later. Once the funeral was over and the household had returned to normal, Mrs McCormack told the family about the wailing she had heard. Her Irish husband suggested that she had heard the banshee. 'Many of my family laughed at this,' Mrs McCormack said. 'They probably thought I was going mad... but I hope never to hear anything like that again.'

The word 'banshee' is derived from the Irish Gaelic term *bean sidhe*, which has the meaning 'woman of the fairies'. Her mournful cry is said to foretell death. According to Irish tradition, she has long red hair and combs it, mermaid-like, as she keens outside the family home of those who are about to die. She is rarely heard or seen by the doomed individual, however.

The banshee has her origins deep in Irish legend. She wailed for ancient heroes such as King Connor McNessa, Finn McCool, and the great Brian Boru, whose victory over the Vikings in 1014 broke their power in Ireland. More recently, residents of the Cork village of Sam's Cross claimed to have heard the eerie voice of the banshee when Michael Collins, commander-in-chief of the Irish Free State Army, was killed in an ambush in 1922 during the Irish Civil War.

'I saw the banshee flying wild in the wind of March': *this is the title of the highly romantic interpretation of the banshee, by Florence Harrison, right.*

In the late 1960s, the Irish psychical researcher Sheila St Clair produced a radio programme for the BBC on the banshee and, even allowing for Irish exaggeration, some of the accounts were chillingly convincing. A baker from Kerry told of an uncomfortable night that he and his colleagues had spent while baking bread ready for the morning delivery.

'It started low at first, then it mounted up into a crescendo; there was definitely some human element in the voice. . . the door to the bakery where I worked was open, too, and the men stopped to listen. Well, it rose as I told you, to a crescendo, and you could almost make out one or two Gaelic words in it; then gradually it went away slowly. Well, we talked about it for a few minutes and at last, coming on to morning, about five o'clock, one of the bread servers came in and he says to me, "I'm afraid

General Michael Collins, commander-in-chief of the Irish Free State Army, top right, was killed in an ambush at Beal-na-Blath – an event that the people of the Cork village of Sam's Cross claimed was foretold by the wailing of a banshee.

The assassination of John F Kennedy, whose funeral is shown right, is said to have been announced to an American businessman and close friend by the cry of the banshee.

they'll need you to take out the cart, for I just got word of the death of an aunt of mine." It was at his cart that the banshee had keened.'

On the same radio programme, an elderly man from County Down tried to describe the particular death cry he had heard in more detail. 'It was a mournful sound,' he said. 'It would have put ye in mind of them ould yard cats on the wall, but it wasn't cats, I know it meself; I thought it was a bird in torment or something. . . a mournful cry it was, and then it was going a wee bit further back, and further until it died away altogether.'

Although *bean sidhe* means literally 'fairy woman', most folklorists classify the banshee as a spirit rather than a 'fairy' or one of the Irish 'little people'; but according to mythology, the banshee will cry at the imminent deaths of fairy kings, too. Some of the older Irish families – the O'Briens and the O'Neils, for example – traditionally regarded the banshee almost as a personal guardian angel, silently watching over the fortunes of the family, guiding its members away from danger, and then performing the final service of 'keening' for their departing souls.

A County Antrim man, meanwhile, told Sheila St Clair, in that same radio programme, his interpretation of the banshee's role. He claimed that, centuries ago, certain of the more pious clans had been blessed with guardian spirits. Because these celestial beings were not able to express themselves in human terms, they were allowed to show their deep feelings only when one of their charges died: the result was the banshee howl. However, said the Antrim man, with the gradual fall from grace of

> **❞** I SAT BOLT UPRIGHT IN BED, AND THE HAIR ON THE BACK OF MY NECK PRICKLED. THE NOISE GOT LOUDER, RISING AND FALLING LIKE AN AIR RAID SIREN. THEN IT DIED AWAY AND I REALISED THAT I WAS TERRIBLY DEPRESSED. I KNEW MY FATHER WAS DEAD. **❞**

the Irish over the years, only the most Godfearing families are privileged to have a death foretold by a personal banshee today.

This theory may please a businessman from Boston, USA, who some years ago claimed that the banshee, like other creatures of European folklore, had crossed the Atlantic. James O'Barry is descended from an Irish family that originally arrived in Massachusetts in 1848. It was as a very small boy that he first heard the banshee.

'I was lying in bed one morning when I heard a weird noise, like a demented woman crying. It was spring, and outside the window the birds were singing, the sun was shining, and the sky was blue. I thought for a moment or two that a wind had sprung up, but a glance at the barely stirring trees told me that this was not so. I went down to breakfast and there was my father sitting at the kitchen table with tears in his eyes. I had never seen him weep before. My mother told me that they had just heard, by telephone, that my grandfather had died in New York. Although he was an old man, he was as fit as a fiddle, and his death was unexpected.'

It was some years before O'Barry learned the legend of the banshee, and then he recalled the wailing noise on the death of his grandfather. In 1946, he heard it again, but in very different circumstances. He was an administrative officer serving with the United States Air Force in the Far East when, one day at 6 a.m., he was awakened by a low howl. He was terrified.

'That time, I was instantly aware of what it was. I sat bolt upright in bed, and the hair on the back of my neck prickled. The noise got louder, rising and falling like an air raid siren. Then it died away, and I realised that I was terribly depressed. I knew my father was dead. A few days later, I had notification that this was so.'

O'Barry was to hear the voice again 17 years later, on what he considers the most remarkable

occasion of all. He was in Toronto, Canada, by himself, enjoying a combined holiday and business trip.

'Again, I was in bed, reading the morning papers, when the dreadful noise was suddenly filling my ears. I thought of my wife, my young son, my two brothers, and I thought: 'Good God, don't let it be one of them.' But for some reason, I knew it wasn't.'

The date was 22 November 1963, the time shortly after noon, and the Irish banshee was bewailing the death of an acquaintance of O'Barry's – President John F. Kennedy.

If the Irish have their banshee, one might reasonably expect their close Celtic cousins, the Scots, to have a version of their own. It is not so, however, although most clans at one time or another have boasted a personal harbinger of death. The nearest thing to the banshee recorded in Scottish folklore are the 'death woman' who sits on westward running streams on the west coast of Scotland, washing the clothes of those about to die, and the Highland 'red fisherman', a robed and hooded apparition who sits angling for fish. To see him is, in itself, the warning of death.

THE DEATH WASH

But the MacLaines of the Isle of Mull, Argyllshire, preserve a curious legend concerning their own death spirit. In the 16th century, Eoghan a' Chin Bhig (Ewan of the Little Head) is said to have had a serious quarrel with his father, MacLaine of Loch Buie. In 1538, both sides collected for a showdown. The evening before the battle, Ewan was out walking when he met an old woman, who was washing a bundle of blood-stained shirts in a stream. Ewan knew that she was a death woman and that the shirts belonged to those who would die in the morning. Rather boldly, he asked if his own shirt

In the 16th century, the chieftain Eoghan (Ewan) a' Chin Bhig was given the island castle of Loch Sguabain, **above,** *as a wedding gift by his father, who lived in Moy Castle,* **right.** *But Ewan, dissatisfied, asked his father for a better castle. A feud resulted, and Ewan was slain in battle. Ever since, the appearance of the headless Ewan has presaged death in the family.*

A banshee appears in a cloud of smoke in the 19th-century illustration, **below.**

THE BANSHEE.

Awful Death warning by the appearance of an Apparition.

was among them, and she said that it was. She told him that if his wife offered him bread and cheese with her own hand, however, he would live and be victorious.

His wife failed to do so. Ewan, demoralised, rode to defeat and, at the height of the battle, a swinging Lochaber axe cut his head clean from his shoulders. His horse galloped off down Glen More, the headless rider still upright in the saddle. According to legend, the dead chief became his own clan's death warning, and his headless body on its galloping horse has been seen three times within living memory just before a family death. The vision is also still believed to herald serious illness whenever it occurs in the family.

Another celebrated Scottish death warning involves the phantom drummer of Cortachy Castle, Tayside, seat of the Earls of Airlie. One story says that he was a Leslie, come to intercede for a truce with his clan's enemies, the Ogilvies – the family name of Airlie – and that he was killed before he could deliver his message. A more romantic version, however, tells that he was a drummer with a Highland regiment and lover of a 15th-century Lady Airlie. He was caught by the Earl and thrown from a turret window.

Four well-attested accounts from the 19th century indicate that the phantom continued to carry

out its warning task efficiently. In the 1840s, the drummer was heard by members of the household before the death of the Countess of Airlie. The Earl married again shortly afterwards, and in 1848 had a house party, the guests including a Miss Margaret Dalrymple. During dinner on her first night, Miss Dalrymple remarked on the curious music she had heard coming from below her window as she dressed – the sound of a fife, followed by drumming. Both her host and hostess paled. After dinner, one of the other guests explained the legend.

GHOSTLY DRUMMING

The following morning, Miss Dalrymple's maid, Ann Day, was alone in the bedroom, attending to her mistress's clothes. She had heard nothing of the drummer story, and so was surprised when she heard a coach draw up in the yard below, accompanied by the sound of drumming. When she realised that the yard was empty though the drumming carried on, she became hysterical. The following day, her mistress heard the sound again, and decided that this was enough. Shortly afterwards, the new Lady Airlie died in Brighton, leaving a note stating that she was sure her death had been signalled by the drumming.

In 1853, several people heard and reported the drummer again, just before the death of the Earl;

> *I* WOULD SUGGEST THAT JUST AS WE INHERIT PHYSICAL CHARACTERISTICS . . . WE ALSO INHERIT MEMORY CELLS . . . AND THOSE OF US WITH STRONG TRIBAL LINEAGES RIDDLED WITH INTERMARRIAGE HAVE THE BANSHEE AS PART OF AN INHERITED MEMORY. *II*
>
> **SHEILA ST CLAIR**

Several accounts testify to the appearance of the phantom drummer of Cortachy Castle, Tayside, above, whenever one of the Ogilvy family is about to die. Two relatives heard the ghostly drumming before the death of David Ogilvy, 10th Earl of Airlie, above left, in 1881.

and in 1881, two relatives told of hearing the prophetic sound while staying at Cortachy during the then Lord Airlie's absence in America. Some days later, news of his death reached them.

In the case of both the Irish banshees and the Scottish death warnings, there are dozens who claim to have heard or seen these harbingers of disaster. Laying aside the unlikely possibility that all of them were either lying or exaggerating, is it possible to explain the phenomenon in any rational way?

Sheila St Clair has an interesting theory that closely relates to psychologist Carl Jung's collective unconscious – an inherited structure of memories passed on from psyche to psyche. 'I would suggest,' she says, 'that just as we inherit physical characteristics . . . we also inherit memory cells, and that those of us with strong tribal lineages riddled with intermarriage have the banshee as part of an inherited memory. The symbolic form of a weeping woman may well be stamped on our racial consciousness.... And just as our other levels of consciousness are not answerable to the limitations of time in our conscious mind, so a particular part of the mind throws up a symbolic hereditary pattern that has in the past been associated with tragedy in the tribe – be it woman, hare, or bird – as a kind of subliminal "four minute warning", so that we may prepare ourselves for that tragedy.'

THE HORROR OF GLAMIS

FOR CENTURIES, GLAMIS CASTLE HAS HAD A REPUTATION AS A PLACE OF STRANGE AND AWFUL HAPPENINGS – EVENTS THAT STRIKE TERROR AT THE HEARTS OF ALL WHO EXPERIENCE THEM

Glamis Castle, picturesque home of the Earl of Strathmore and Kinghorne, below, was a wedding gift from King Robert II upon the marriage of his daughter to Sir John Lyon in the 14th century. From the time that Sir John moved to Glamis, the family seems to have been dogged by misfortune.

The painting of the Third Earl, Patrick, with his children and greyhounds, right, dominates the far wall of the drawing room at Glamis. It is around Patrick that two strange stories revolve.

Malcolm II, above, reigned as King of Scotland from 1005 until his death at Glamis in 1034, at the hands of an army of rebels. Tradition holds that he was slain in what is now known as King Malcolm's Room, top right, and that his brutal murder saw the start of the 'horror' at the castle.

Glamis Castle stands in the great vale of Strathmore in Tayside, Scotland. For centuries, the vast fortified house with its battlements and pointed towers – looking very much like the setting for a fairy tale – has been the home of the Earls of Strathmore. Their family secret is reputedly hidden within the walls of Glamis, famous as one of the most haunted houses on earth.

That there was some form of unpleasantness within the castle's walls is an undoubted historical fact. And that the castle is today the centre of a triangle formed by three biblically named villages – Jericho, Zoar, and Pandanaram – may indicate the terror felt by its minions; for, according to a Scottish National Trust guidebook, the men who built and named them 'had at least some knowledge of the Scriptures and regard for the wrath of God'. That wrath, claim locals, was called down on Glamis for the sins of the first dozen or so lairds. In recent times, however, there is little to suggest that life at the castle has been anything other than pleasant and peaceful. While Michael Fergus Bowes-Lyon, the 18th, and present, Earl is well-liked by his tenants, as were his immediate forbears, the conduct of at least one of their ancestors called into being what became known as the 'horror' of Glamis.

It is the obscure nature of the horror that makes accounts of it all the more terrifying. Indeed, no recent Earl has ever spoken of it to an outsider, except in enigmatic terms, and no woman has ever been let in on the secret. It is passed on only to the Strathmore heir on his 21st birthday.

The historical record of horror at Glamis Castle goes back to 1034, when King Malcolm II was cut down by a gang of rebellious subjects armed with claymores, the large broadswords peculiar to Scotland. It was said that every drop of Malcolm's blood seeped from his body into the floorboards, causing a stain that is still pointed out today, in what is called King Malcolm's Room. That the stain was made by Malcolm's blood is disputable, how-

ever, for records seem to show that the flooring has since been replaced. Nevertheless, Malcolm's killers added to the death toll of Glamis by trying to escape across a frozen loch: but the ice cracked and they were drowned.

CURSE OF THE CHALICE

The Lyon family inherited Glamis from King Robert II, who gave it to his son-in-law, Sir John Lyon, in 1372. Until then, the Lyon family home had been at Forteviot, where a great chalice, the family 'luck', was kept. Tradition held that if the chalice were removed from Forteviot House, a curse would fall on the family. Despite this, Sir John took the cup with him to Glamis. The curse, though, seems to have had a time lapse: Sir John was indeed killed in a duel, but this did not occur until 1383, and the family misfortunes are usually dated from this time.

The 'poisoned' chalice may well have also influenced events 150 years later when James V had Janet Douglas, Lady Glamis, burned at the stake in Edinburgh on a charge of witchcraft. The castle reverted to the Crown; but after the falsity of the charge was proved, Glamis was restored to her son. The spectre of Lady Glamis – the 'Grey Lady' as she is known – is said regularly to walk the long corridors even today.

It was Patrick, the Third Earl of Strathmore, who made the idea of a Glamis 'curse' widespread in the late 17th century: indeed, to many people he seemed the very embodiment of it. A notorious rake and gambler, he was known in both London and Edinburgh, as well as throughout his home territory, for his drunken debauchery. Facts covering his career and his character are festooned with folklore, but he must have been something of an enigma; for despite his wild ways, he was philanthropic towards his tenants at least. The *Glamis Book of Record*, for instance, details his plans for building a group of lodges on the estate for the use of retired workers. Now known as Kirkwynd Cottages, they were given to the Scottish National Trust by the 16th Earl of Strathmore in 1957, to house the Angus Folk Collection.

Two principal stories endure about Patrick. The first is that he was the father of a deformed child who was kept hidden somewhere in the castle, out of sight of prying eyes. The second is that he played cards with the Devil for his soul – and lost.

The first story is fed by a picture of the Third Earl that now hangs in the drawing room. It shows Patrick seated, wearing a classical bronze breastplate, and pointing with his left hand towards a distant, romanticised vista of Glamis. Standing at his left knee is a small, strange-looking, green-clad child; to the child's left is an upright young man in scarlet doublet and hose. The three main figures are placed centrally, but two greyhounds in the picture are shown staring steadfastly at a figure, positioned at the Earl's right elbow. Like the Earl, this figure wears a classical breastplate, apparently shaped to the muscles of the torso – but if it is a human torso, it is definitely deformed. The left arm is also strangely foreshortened. Did the artist paint from life – and if so, does the picture show the real 'horror' of Glamis?

DIABOLICAL GAMES

The second story goes like this. Patrick and his friend the Earl of Crawford were playing cards together one Saturday night when a servant reminded them that the Sabbath was approaching. Patrick replied that he would play, Sabbath or no Sabbath, and that the Devil himself might join them for a hand if he so wished. At midnight, accompanied by a roll of thunder, the Devil appeared and told the card-playing Earls that they had forfeited their souls and were therefore doomed to play cards in that room until Judgement Day.

The pact presumably came into operation only after Patrick's death, and there is some evidence that he revelled in the tale. But did he tell it merely as a joke or as some sort of elaborate cover up, in order to scare intruders forever from the castle? If the latter was his intention, it was certainly strikingly successful. In 1957, a servant at the castle, Florence Foster, complained in a newspaper article that she had heard the Earls at their play in the dead of night, 'rattling dice, stamping and swearing. Often I lay in bed and shook with fright,' she said, and resigned rather than risk hearing the phantom gamblers again. The story persists even today of a secret room known only to the Earls themselves, and no one knows for certain which of the hundred-odd rooms at Glamis was used by Patrick for his diabolical game of cards.

Another story tells – with curious precision – of a grey-bearded man, shackled and left to starve in 1486. A later one, probably also dating from before Patrick's time, is gruesome in the extreme. A party of Ogilvies from a neighbouring district came to Glamis and begged protection from their enemies, the Lindsays, who were pursuing them. The Earl of Strathmore led them into a chamber, deep in the castle, and left them there to starve. Unlike the unfortunate grey-bearded man, however, they had each other to eat and began to turn cannibal – some, according to legend, even gnawing the flesh from their own arms.

Lady Elizabeth Bowes-Lyon, below, who was to become Queen Mother, grew up at Glamis. She is said to have felt the presence of what was possibly the 'horror' in the Blue Room.

One or other of these tales may account for a skeletally thin spectre, known as Jack the Runner; and the ghost of a black pageboy, also seen in the castle, seems to date from the 17th or 18th century, when young slaves were imported from the West Indies. A 'white' lady is also said to haunt the castle clock tower, while the grey-bearded man of 1486 appeared, at least once, to two guests simultaneously, one of whom was the wife of the Archbishop of York at the turn of the 20th century. She told how, during her stay at the castle, one of the guests came down to breakfast and mentioned casually that she had been awakened by the banging and hammering of carpenters at 4 a.m. A brief silence followed her remarks, and then Lord Strathmore spoke, assuring her that there were no workmen in the castle. According to another story, as a young girl, Queen Elizabeth, the Queen Mother (daughter of the 14th Earl, Claude George Bowes-Lyon), once had to move out of the Blue Room because her sleep was being disturbed by rappings, thumps, and footsteps.

Fascinating as all these run-of-the-mill ghosts and their distinguished observers are, however, it is

the 'horror' that remains the great mystery of Glamis. All the principal rumours – cannibal Ogilvies notwithstanding – involve a deformed child, born to the family and kept in a secret chamber, who lived, according to 19th-century versions of the story, to a very old age. In view of the portrait openly displayed at Glamis, and always supposing that it is the mysterious child who is actually portrayed, subsequent secrecy seems rather pointless. If Patrick himself was prepared to have his 'secret' portrayed in oils, why should successors have discouraged open discussion of the matter?

UNMENTIONABLE HORROR

Despite the secrecy, at the turn of the 19th century, stories were still flying thick and fast. Claude Bowes-Lyon, the 13th Earl who died in 1904 in his 80th year, seems to have been positively obsessed by the horror, and it is around him that most of the 19th-century stories revolved. It was he, for instance, who told an inquisitive friend: 'If you could guess the nature of the secret, you would go down on your knees and thank God it were not yours.' Claude, too, it was who paid the passage of a workman and his family to Australia, after the workman had inadvertently stumbled upon a 'secret room' at Glamis and been overcome with horror. Claude questioned him, swore the man to secrecy, and bundled him off to the colonies shortly afterwards. To a great extent, the obsession seems to have visited itself upon his son, Claude George, the 14th Earl, who died in 1944.

In the 1920s, a party of young people staying at Glamis decided to track down the 'secret chamber' by hanging a piece of linen out of every window they could find. When they finished, they saw there were several windows that they had not been able to locate from the inside. When the Earl learned what they had done, he flew into an uncharacteristic fury. Unlike his forbears, however, Claude George broke the embargo on the secret by telling it to his estate factor, Gavin Ralston, who subsequently refused to stay overnight at the castle again.

The 13th Earl of Strathmore, Claude Bowes-Lyon, seen left, was deeply troubled by the tales of strange events at Glamis. The wife of the Archbishop of York wrote that: 'For many years, after the revelation of the secret, Claude was quite a changed man, silent and moody, with an anxious, scared look on his face. So evident was the effect on him that his son, Glamis, when he came of age in 1876, absolutely refused to be enlightened.'

It was in the chapel at Glamis, below left, that a secret room was discovered in the late 19th century. A workman came upon the door by chance and, finding that it led into a long passage, decided to investigate – but he soon emerged, shaking with fright. He reported his experience to the Earl who, anxious to preserve the family secret, persuaded the man to emigrate.

When the 14th Earl's daughter-in-law, the next Lady Strathmore, asked Ralston the secret, Ralston is said to have replied: 'It is lucky that you do not know and can never know it, for if you did, you would not be a happy woman.'

That statement, surely, is the clue to the horror of Glamis. Old Patrick's deformed offspring did not alarm the father because nothing like it had been seen in the family before. Possibly the 'wicked' Earl rather delighted in him. But if the same deformity appeared even once in a later generation, the head of an ancient, noble and hereditary house would certainly have been reluctant to broadcast the fact. Perhaps Claude, 13th Earl of Strathmore, knew of such a second, deformed child in the Bowes-Lyon line, and passed the secret, and the fear of its recurrence, on to his successors?

" IF YOU COULD GUESS THE NATURE OF THE SECRET, YOU WOULD GO DOWN ON YOUR KNEES AND THANK GOD IT WERE NOT YOURS. "

CLAUDE BOWES-LYON

PERSPECTIVES
THE HAUNTED HIGHLANDS

The Highlands of Scotland abound in tales of ghosts and supernatural incidents. Given the number of castles in the region – and the bloody fighting they must have seen during their long histories – it is not surprising that many are associated with gruesome events. One story concerns Duntrune Castle in Argyll, which in the 17th century was about to be attacked by a chieftain called 'Left-handed Coll'. Before he did so, he sent his piper to do a bit of spying, but the man was discovered and shut up in a turret room. However, he managed to warn his chief by playing *The Piper's Warning to his Master*, whereupon Campbell of Duntrune chopped off both his hands. In recent years, two skeleton hands were found under the kitchen floor, and the piper's ghost and tune is said still to haunt the tower.

Amid the ruins of Dunphail Castle, a few miles south of Forres, in the Grampian region of northern Scotland, visitors have claimed to hear the sounds of battle and to have seen the spectral, severed heads of several men. In a previous century, apparently, the men had escaped from the castle while it was under siege, and then hurled sacks of grain over the wall to starving members of their clan. The men were soon captured and beheaded, and their heads thrown over the walls, accompanied by the chilling cry: 'Here's beef for your bannocks (bread)!'

A young girl's pride, meanwhile, lies behind the haunting of Castle Grant, near Grantown-on-Spey, 20 miles (32 kilometres) south of Forres, in the Highland region. The ghost is believed to be the spirit of a certain Barbara Grant, who has been seen washing her hands in a bedroom in the tower, then rushing across the room to the staircase. It is said that, in the 16th-century, her father had locked her up in the tower because she refused to marry a man he had chosen for her, but whom she did not love. And there, in the tower, she eventually died – only her agitated ghost still supposedly reliving her sad fate.

A GUILT-RIDDEN GHOST

Frendraught House, left, was the family seat of the powerful Crichton clan for many years. Because of the tragedy that took place there in the 17th century, it is said to be haunted even today.

Part of the original old tower staircase at Frendraught, below, is the scene of a modern-day haunting.

THE SPECTRE OF THE LADY OF THE MANOR STILL HAUNTS THE SCENE OF A FIRE THAT KILLED SEVERAL MEMBERS OF ONE FACTION – A FIRE FOR WHICH THE LOCAL POPULACE HAD HELD HER TO BE ULTIMATELY RESPONSIBLE

One of the classic themes of supernatural lore is the unhappy ghost, doomed to haunt the scene of its earthly wrongdoing until its sins are expiated. Could Frendraught House in Aberdeenshire, Scotland, be just such a scene of a 'penitential' haunting? There are folklorists and witnesses who think that it is.

The building lies about 6 miles (9 kilometres) to the east of Huntly in the centre of the extensive Bognie estates. Its foundations date from 1203, though additions were made to it as recently as the 1840s. Its main bulk – containing inner walls up to 9 feet (2.7 metres) thick – was built between the 14th and 17th centuries, when it was both home and fortress to the powerful Crichton family. During those three centuries, the Crichtons, along with their cousins and neighbours, the Gordons and

Leslies, controlled the north-east of Scotland. And the whole family was often embroiled in bloody feuds with rival clans.

In the spring of 1630, Frendraught was occupied by Sir James Crichton. He had made a good political marriage to Lady Elizabeth Gordon, eldest daughter of the Earl of Sutherland, and she took an active part in her husband's continual disputes. As one Victorian commentator put it, she played a role somewhere between that of Medusa and Lady Macbeth.

The 1630 dispute over boundary lands had arisen between Sir James Crichton and Gordon, Laird of Rothiemay. Sir James settled it in typical fashion – by shooting Gordon dead. The Marquis of Huntly, the local High Sheriff, who was himself a Gordon, and closely related to both sides, fined Sir James heavily. This 'blood money' was paid to young John Gordon, the new Laird of Rothiemay, and honour seemed satisfied.

By midsummer, however, Sir James was fighting again, this time with Leslie of Pitcaple. Matters came to a head when a Crichton shot Leslie through the arm with an arrow. Again, the Marquis of Huntly heard the case, this time ruling in favour of Sir James. The wounded Leslie rode off in a fury, openly swearing revenge on the house of Crichton. Sir James therefore took the precaution of assembling an armed party to escort him back to Frendraught. Surprisingly, it included young John Gordon of Rothiemay, as well as the Marquis of Huntly's son, John Melgum Viscount Aboyne.

The party arrived in the dusk of an October afternoon. Lady Crichton, perhaps relieved to see her husband home safely, pressed even the unloved

Among the guests of Sir James and Lady Elizabeth Crichton, seen right and below, were some clan rivals who met death by fire at Frendraught House. Lady Crichton was known to be a strong support to Sir James in his many feuds – which may be why people thought her guilty of causing the fire.

The Marquis of Huntly, below right, the local High Sheriff, was closely involved in the events at Frendraught House – not just as an official. His son, Lord Melgum, was one of those who burned to death in the old tower while trying to help the others.

'When he stood at the wire window
Most doleful to be seen
He did espy the Lady Frendraught
Who stood upon the green.
And mercy, mercy Lady Frendraught
Will ye not sink with sin
For first your husband kilt my father
And now ye burn his son.
Oh, then it spake Lady Frendraught
And loudly did she cry
It was great pity for good Lord John
But none for Rothiemay
But the keys are sunk in the deep draw well
Ye cannot get away.'

To the Marquis of Huntly, there was only one way to avenge his dead son. Laying aside his High Sheriff's impartiality, he recruited a small army of highlanders and raided Frendraught, carrying off 60 cattle and several dozen sheep.

Crichton appealed to Edinburgh, and the Privy Council came down in his favour. Huntly was fined and Sir James received damages.

Despite their vindication by the Privy Council, both Sir James and his Lady seemed changed by the terrible fire. Three years afterwards, Sir James gave a silver chalice, said to have been one of 11 brought north by Mary Queen of Scots, to the nearby kirk at Forgue. Today, the chalice, the oldest known piece of hallmarked silver in Scotland, lies in a bank vault in Huntly.

Lady Frendraught took her three daughters and went to live as a recluse at Kinnairdy on the River

Gordon kin to stay the night. The guests were put in the old tower.

Lord Melgum was given a room that was separated from the upper storeys by a wooden staircase. John Gordon of Rothiemay was on the second floor, and the other guests and servants had accommodation above him. Spalding, a contemporary chronicler, tells what happened that tragic night: 'About midnight that dolorous tower took fire in so sudden and furious a manner, and in ane clap, that the noble Viscount, the Laird of Rothiemay, English Will, Colonel Ivat and others, servants, were cruelly burned and tormented to death.'

Lord Melgum, it is said, ran to help the others, but the wooden stair caught fire and he was trapped with them. According to Spalding: 'They hurried to the window looking out into the close, piteously calling for help, but none was or could be rendered them.' Altogether, about a dozen people lost their lives.

DEATH BY DESIGN

An event of this magnitude cast shadows far beyond north-east Scotland, and the Privy Council in Edinburgh soon became involved, setting up a commission of bishops and neutral peers to investigate the death of so many. The commission sat at Frendraught on 13 April 1631. However, the bishops merely declared that 'the fire could not have happened accidentally but designedly.' There the mystery of the fire rests, unsolved to this day. However, local opinion of the time laid the blame squarely on Lady Frendraught. An anonymous ballad, written a few months after the event, said of Rothiemay's final moments:

Deveron. Born a Catholic, she was excommunicated when she signed the Solemn League and Covenant supporting Presbyterianism. Subsequently wanting to turn back to her old faith, she was rebuffed. 'I refused absolutely to see her,' wrote Father Blackhall, 'because she was suspected to be guilty of the death of my Lord Aboyne... ' When she died, it was without benefit of clergy, and on an unrecorded date. She was buried, like her husband, in an unmarked grave.

Sir James' eldest son was the last of his line. He was created Viscount Frendraught by his cousin Charles I for services rendered during the Civil War. After his death, his widow married George Morison of that Ilk, Chief of the Morison Clan and Laird of Bognie. His descendant, Alexander Gordon Morison, became Laird of Bognie and Mountblairy, and owner of Frendraught House in 1942. He was born in Canada, and inherited the chieftainship and family estates from his uncle. Immediately after the Second World War, he and his young family lived at Frendraught House, but later moved to Mountblairy – not, he insisted, for fear of ghosts, but for practical reasons.

'According to local opinion and the direct testimony of tenants, guests, and my wife,' said Mr Morison, 'Frendraught is haunted by Lady Elizabeth Crichton, who is bound there because of her guilt. I have never felt or seen anything myself, but according to legend the Laird never does anyway.' Mr Morison expressed a firm belief in Lady Crichton's guilt. He even cited documents showing that, when the 'deep draw well' in the courtyard was cleaned out during alterations in the 1840s, massive keys were found. This, of course, supports the allegations of the old ballad.

PALE-FACED INTRUDER

The recorded sightings of a 'dark woman in a white dress' at Frendraught go back at least to the early 18th century when a Victorian clergyman-writer claimed that she was seen both in the house and among the great beeches around it. The first modern sighting on record occurred in 1938, at a time when the house stood empty and locked. The late William Thomas, former manager of Glendronough Distillery on the borders of the Bognie estate, was in his early teens at the time. One autumn afternoon, he was out shooting crows behind the house. Looking up, he saw a pale face surrounded by dark hair, watching him from a window overlooking the courtyard. He called a keeper who also saw the 'intruder'. Armed with their shotguns, the two broke in through a kitchen door and searched the

"...IF THERE IS INDEED A TENDENCY FOR THE PLACES FREQUENTED BY A HAUNTING APPARITION TO BE ALSO THE SCENES OF PECULIAR PHYSICAL HAPPENINGS... THIS MUST SURELY STRENGTHEN THE VIEW THAT HAUNTING APPARITIONS EITHER ARE, OR ARE IN SOME WAY PRODUCED BY, LOCALIZED AND OBJECTIVE ENTITIES OR FACTORS."

ALAN GAULD,

MEDIUMSHIP AND SURVIVAL

The ghost of Lady Frendraught, in a white-and-gold dress, has been seen on the main staircase of Frendraught House, left, as well as in the grounds of the estate.

The silver chalice, opposite below, was presented to Forgue Kirk by Sir James, three years after the fire. It is said to have been brought to Scotland by Mary Queen of Scots and is the oldest piece of hallmarked silver in the country.

house from top to bottom. There was nobody there, and no sign of forcible entry could be found but their own.

Nearly 10 years later, Mrs Yvonne Morison encountered the ghost.

'It was 28 October. I remember the date because my husband had gone away with the Canadian Army reserve the day before. I was completely alone in the kitchens in the basement – the oldest part. Suddenly, in the silence, I heard footsteps coming down the staircase from the top of the house. I was terrified, but something made me

Yvonne and Alexander Gordon Morison, above and left, became owners of Frendraught House in 1942. Here, Mrs Morison had a personal encounter with a ghost, believed to be that of Lady Crichton – as did guests and subsequent tenants.

go to the bottom of the stairs where they eventually entered the kitchen. I peered up into the darkness and remember thinking very strongly – I may even have spoken aloud – 'Well, come on then. If you exist, show yourself!' Perhaps fortunately, the footfalls stopped at the top of the kitchen stairs, and I saw and heard nothing else.'

The footsteps were too heavy and clear to be made by mice, she said, and rats had never been seen in the building. 'I knew all the "natural" creaks and groans of the old place. It was none of these.'

Twice, the Morisons had guests who cut short their visits because of mysterious disturbances that made them feel uncomfortable. On both occasions, the guests were level-headed people. One was an old army colleague who had been in the thick of the fighting with Mr Morison during the Italian campaign. In both cases, their stories matched in every detail, though they had never met. Mrs Morison explained:

'It was quite funny at first. They were a bit embarrassed, and it became clear that they thought my husband and I had begun a furious fight during the night. When we pointed out that the wall between our bedroom and theirs was 8 feet [2,4 metres] thick and totally soundproof, they became alarmed. They said that they had heard the most dreadful cries for help, with the sound of crashing, like heavy furniture being thrown about, and screams. They had been too terrified to investigate.'

CURSE OF THE CHALICE

Several guests and subsequent tenants at Frendraught had described seeing a dark lady in a white dress that was edged and decorated in gold. She was usually standing or walking on the main staircase or the back stairs.

Cryle Shand – genealogist, lawyer, and tenant of Yonder Bognie Farm – admitted to having an open mind on the subject of the ghost, but felt that Lady Crichton was more to be pitied than blamed. According to his own theory, she may have been impelled to whatever action she took by a curse – the curse, perhaps, of the chalice that Sir James gave to Forgue Kirk three years after the fire, and that now lies in a bank vault.

'From my research, I am almost certain that the cup was one of those brought north by Mary Queen of Scots in the middle of the 16th century: although it is hallmarked 1663, its base is typically pre-Reformation. The Bible says that "he that eateth and drinketh unworthily, eateth and drinketh damnation unto himself." Although the Crichtons were nominally a Catholic family, they were a fairly ungodly lot. I believe that Sir James used the sacred chalice for profane purposes – probably for drinking his dram out of – and that the troubles of his family, and those of the Gordons who were so closely related to them, were brought about by Biblical damnation. That is why Crichton so piously repented and gave the cup back to the Church. That is why it is treated with such respect by the elders of Forgue Kirk to this day. And that is why Dr Arthur Johnson, an 18th-century Scottish Latinist, describes Frendraught as *Tristis et infelix et semper inhospita turris* ('A sad and unhappy and ever inhospitable tower.')'

POLTERGEIST PARADOXES

ARE THERE REAL, PHYSICAL POWERS THAT LIE BEHIND THE ACTIVITIES OF POLTERGEISTS, OR DO SUCH UNNERVING EFFECTS STEM SIMPLY FROM THE SUBCONSCIOUS MIND?

In 1952, researchers investigating poltergeist activity witnessed a remarkable incident. The heavy oak table around which they were sitting suddenly tilted slightly and rose – apparently of its own accord. It then moved forward over the floor, pushing ahead of it two of the men, both of whom were tall and well-built.

They were pushed into the fireplace behind them and, although unharmed, were considerably surprised. No external cause could be found for this incident, yet they noted that the temperature in the room had dropped dramatically, and one of the group (who was only later discovered to be a psychic) appeared to be in a trance-state. Such events have, it seems, been observed on countless other occasions, and in many parts of the world.

Certain physiological reactions to such phenomena have also been observed, recorded and measured. Loss of weight can sometimes occur, for instance. One medium, Eusapia Palladino (1854-1918), even claimed that she shed 20 pounds (9 kilograms) during a single seance. Experiments in Ireland with a table weighing 30 pounds (13.6 kilograms), wired up to equipment monitoring its weight, showed that when it was levitated, it somehow 'lost' 15 pounds. Unfortunately, a more thorough examination of weight-loss during such activities is extremely difficult, because there is usually no warning that an episode is about to occur.

The rapid drop in temperature that was noticed in the 1952 case also occurs in spontaneous phenomena of other sorts, records testifying to a fall of as much as 8°C (4.4°F) in 10 seconds. This sudden loss of heat apparently releases a great deal of energy, which may well account not only for the blue sparks that some witnesses claim to see, but also the malfunction of electrical equipment that is often observed. Lights, televisions and cookers are at times reported to turn themselves on and off as may, ironically, the monitoring equipment of researchers.

Electrical charges definitely seem to be a measurable by-product of psychokinesis. In an

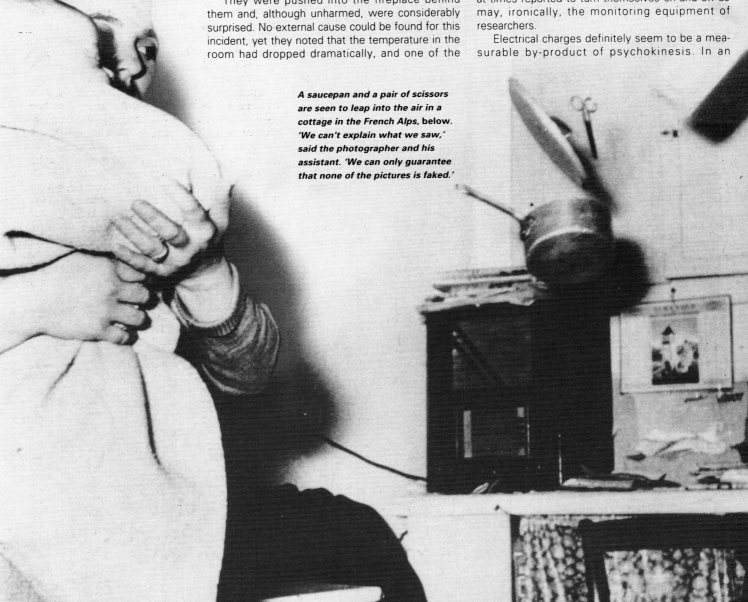

A saucepan and a pair of scissors are seen to leap into the air in a cottage in the French Alps, below. 'We can't explain what we saw,' said the photographer and his assistant. 'We can only guarantee that none of the pictures is faked.'

experiment carried out in Folkestone, Kent, for instance, it was established that a group of seven people, sitting at a table with hands joined, was able to generate a considerable electrical charge that lasted for three seconds. And in the case of 'Philip, the Imaginary Ghost', a group was able to produce recordable and apparently intelligent raps from the table, despite the fact that the entity was entirely 'fictional'. Hyperventilation is another phenomenon often encountered in such situations, mediums frequently seen to experience deep and rapid breathing as they enter a state of trance.

The psychological causes or effects of poltergeist activity are less easy to measure, though many victims display the same symptoms and have similar experiences. Many see apparitions, some of which are replicas of living people and some thought to be hallucinatory images – although they may be apparitions of unrecognised people. At the time when the Enfield poltergeist case was being investigated, the 'ghost' of Maurice Grosse, one of the researchers, was seen in the house at least twice. Dozens of other reports confirm that such an experience is not uncommon, though by no means all claims have been substantiated by evidence. But it does seem that it is often necessary for the poltergeist victim to create a visible form for the invisible agent of the disturbances, in order to be able to cope with the phenomenon. In other words, the 'ghost' provides an excuse for the disturbance, so that responsibility for damage can be placed on its phantom shoulders. In some instances, an apparition is seen even before a psychokinetic incident takes place, as though it were the catalyst or agent. As poltergeist activity frequently erupts when tension or trauma is experi-

The famous Italian medium, Eusapia Palladino, is shown above, raising a table about 10 inches (25 centimetres) above the floor. During a demonstration of this sort, she claimed that she would lose as much as 20 pounds (9 kilograms) in weight.

A table was seen to levitate in front of television cameras, below, during a seance in which 'Philip', the imaginary phantom, was 'contacted'.

enced, the appearance of a 'ghost' may itself be a symptom of stress; and the shock caused by the appearance of such a mysterious figure may then trigger a series of inexplicable events for which the 'ghost' is blamed.

CONVERSION NEUROSIS

Neurosis is another psychological condition associated with psychokinesis. Indeed, Professor A. R. G. Owen suggested that 'poltergeistry' may actually be a conversion neurosis. In certain people, in other words, acute anxiety may be converted into noise and the movement of objects. But, if that is the case, why does poltergeist activity cease? 'Maybe', Professor Owen theorised, 'the activity eventually ends because it is not a disease but the cure.' Sleepwalking, another symptom of deep anxiety, is also associated with victims of poltergeist activity. It seems that the activity often continues while the victim is asleep, which supports the theory that the unconscious mind is the true source of the power. Mary Carrick, an Irish girl living in America in 1898, was 'pursued' by raps on the walls of rooms in which she worked, and heavy objects would move in her presence. She would often carry out housework while still asleep, and the knockings would continue unabated. Taps and scratchings have also been heard near beds in other cases, even when the victims were sound asleep.

A series of laboratory tests conducted on a housewife in the Soviet Union in the 1970 revealed the extent to which physiological and psychological factors collaborate to produce psychokinetic forces. Among other things, Nina Kulagina was able to separate the yolk of an egg from the white, and then reassemble the egg, without touching the container in which it had been placed. She was also able to arrest the heartbeat of a frog by suppressing an electric current. (She was not even told that the wires carrying the current were connected to a living creature.) In other tests, small electrodes were attached to her head and recording apparatus to her heart and wrists so that electrical pulses, generated during psychokinetic incidents, could be monitored.

Tests proved that the electrical activity of her brain rose to a very high level at such times, and that her pulse rate increased to an incredible 240

activity; she experienced slight dizziness; and her sleep pattern was disturbed. The sugar content of her blood increased, and her pulse rate became erratic. (Practically identical symptoms have been observed in people suffering from a mild form of epilepsy and also in certain women who are going through the menopause.)

LINGERING ENERGY

The generation of psychokinetic power thus appears to have its origins in certain psychological conditions, to which physiological symptoms bear witness. Yet the power seems to have an existence that is independent, to some extent, of those who generate it. A concentration of energy, once it is consciously created, also appears to linger in selected areas. In 1973, for example, it was discovered that a compass needle, deflected by psychokinetic force, would continue to oscillate if placed in the area in which a sensitive had originally projected the power, despite the fact that she was no longer present. One researcher, William Roll, even claimed that if one disturbance had taken place in a given area, another disturbance was likely to occur there.

beats a minute. (A rate of about 70 is considered normal.) The magnetic field around Kulagina also increased significantly; and when all the electrical and electromagnetic forces reached their peak, they merged in a single, fluctuating rhythm. At this point, she was able to move objects at some distance from her without touching them in any way. During each successful trial in which her psychokinetic power was evident, Kulagina is reported to have lost 4 pounds (1.8 kilograms).

The continuous monitoring of the woman's physical condition provided proof that Nina Kulagina was in a state of considerable nervous tension. An electroencephalograph registered intense brain

A table is levitated by English medium Jack Webber, during a seance, above.

The Polish medium Stanislawa Tomczyk demonstrates the levitation of small objects in full daylight, right. After her marriage in 1919, she gave up all practices of this kind, and claimed that her 'act' had indeed been fraudulent – but she never explained how it was done.

PERSPECTIVES
SUBSTANCE OF THE SPIRIT

Ectoplasm was originally a biological term, meaning the outer layer of the cell protoplasm. But in 1905, the French physiologist and psychical researcher Charles Richet lent the name to 'a kind of liquid paste or jelly [that] emerges from the mouth or breast...[and] organises itself by degrees, acquiring the shape of a face or limb.'

In the cases described by Juliette Bisson in her book *Phénomènes dits de Matérialisation,* the most stringent precautions produced no evidence of fraud, and investigators were unable to determine the nature of the substance. However, in the many instances of ectoplasmic materialisation that have been recorded since 1905, the phenomenon is generally suspect.

Mediums insist that ectoplasm is a living substance, which is destroyed by exposure to light; but interestingly, since the availability of infra-red film, there have been very few claims for the production of ectoplasm.

In photographs that were obtained during the 1920s and 30s, 'ectoplasm' bears a close resemblance to butter muslin – indeed, one of the only two specimens of ectoplasm ever obtained was found to be of this material: the other was of chewed lavatory paper. The fetid smell so often associated with ectoplasm also indicates, some believe, that it could have emerged from concealment within one of the body's orifices.

The idea that a 'cosmic force' lies behind those inexplicable incidents that are categorised as poltergeist activity is at least four centuries old. Paracelsus is believed to have proposed this explanation in the 16th century; and Mesmer, the celebrated hypnotist, promoted the belief some 300 years later. Today, experts in the field of parapsychology are extremely reluctant to concede any ground to the theory. Indeed, it is generally acknowledged that psychokinesis is a form of 'thought force', the origins of which are natural rather than supernatural. As Scott Rogo so neatly put it in a paper in the *Journal of the Society for Psychical Research:* 'Psychokinesis is a phenomenon of vast contradictions. It seems to be both a mental and a physical force at one and the same time.' At present, an explanation for the phenomenon lies beyond the boundaries of scientific theory. General acceptance and a deeper understanding of the force in the future will doubtless depend on strictly controlled investigation of psychokinesis in all its forms.

THE IMAGE OF SOMEONE TURNING INTO A WOLF IS ONE THAT HAS HAUNTED HUMAN IMAGINATION FOR CENTURIES. IT FINDS ITS CHIEF EXPRESSION IN THE TERRIFYING LEGEND OF THE WEREWOLF. BUT COULD THERE BE MORE TO SUCH TALES THAN MERE SUPERSTITION?

HOWLS OF HORROR

Towards the middle of the 19th century, on a picturesque hill near the Vistula, a river in Poland that flows past Cracow and Warsaw, a large gathering of young people were celebrating, with music, singing and dancing, the completion of the harvest. There was food and drink in abundance, and everyone indulged freely.

Suddenly, while the merry-making was in full swing, a terrible, blood-curdling cry echoed across the valley. Abandoning their dancing, the young men and women ran in the direction from which the cry had come and discovered, to their horror, that an enormous wolf had seized one of the village's prettiest girls, recently engaged to be married, and was dragging her away. Her fiancé was nowhere to be seen.

The most courageous of the men went in pursuit of the wolf and eventually confronted it. But the furious monster, its mouth foaming with a fiendish rage, dropped its human prey on the ground and stood over it, ready to fight. Some of the villagers ran home to fetch guns and axes; but the wolf, seeing the fear of those who remained, again seized the girl and vanished into the nearby forest.

Many years elapsed; and then, at another harvest feast, on the same hill, an old man approached the revellers. They invited him to join in the celebrations, but the old man, gloomy and reserved, chose to sit down to drink in silence. A countryman of roughly the same age then joined him and, after looking at him closely for a moment or two, asked with some emotion: 'Is it you, John?'

The old man nodded, and instantly the countryman recognised the stranger as his older brother, who had disappeared many years before. The merry-makers quickly gathered round the old visitor and listened to his strange tale. He told them how, having been changed into a wolf by a sorcerer, he had carried his fiancée away from that same hill during a harvest festival and had lived with her in the nearby forest for a year, after which she died.

'From that moment on', he continued, 'savage and furious, I attacked every man, woman and child, and destroyed every animal I came across. My trail

The lonely figure of a wolf, above, gives its blood-curdling howl. Although stories of men taking on the forms of other beasts – such as werebears, or werehyenas – exist, werewolf tales are by far the most common in Europe, probably because the wolf was one of the most vicious and powerful animals known to Man.

of bloodshed I cannot even now completely wipe away.' At this point he showed them his hands, which were covered with bloodstains.

'It is some four years since, having once again changed back to human shape, I have wandered from place to place. I wanted to see you all once more – to see the cottage and village where I was born and grew up to be a man. After that... well, I shall become a wolf again.'

No sooner had he uttered these words than he changed into a wolf. He rushed past the astonished onlookers and disappeared into the forest, never to be seen again.

The fairy-tale aspects of this story make it very difficult to take seriously. Could too much drink have enhanced the already colourful imagination of the peasant folk? Could detail have been built upon detail with each new telling until the story reached

BORN TO BE WILD

The French anthropologist, Jean-Claude Armen, has reported that on several occasions during the 1970s he saw a 'human gazelle' in the Syrian desert.

The creature, was a 10-year-old boy who galloped 'in gigantic bounds amongst a long cavalcade of white gazelles'. According to Armen, this 'gazelle boy' seemed to have adapted himself to the life of the herd, licking and sniffing at the animals in the friendliest of ways.

This seemingly well-authenticated account is just one example of many reports dating back to the Middle Ages of encounters with human children who have supposedly been reared by wild animals.

The most frequently-featured foster-parents in such accounts are wolves – animals that haunted the ancient forests of Europe and beyond, and that became a staple element of folk tales.

One of the earliest of wolf stories is that of Romulus and Remus, the legendary founders of Rome, who as babies were suckled by a she-wolf. In modern times, however, one of the most intriguing cases of children supposedly reared by wolves occurred in India in 1920. Two girls, aged two and eight, were allegedly found in a wolf-lair at Midnapore in West Bengal by an Anglican clergyman, the Reverend J.A.L. Singh.

Singh kept a diary of his efforts to humanise the two, whom he named Amala and Kamala. Civilising them proved a difficult task, for they ran on all fours, howled like wolves, and ate only raw meat. The younger child, Amala, died within a year of being found, but Kamala lived for a further nine years, learning to walk upright and to speak over 30 words.

It remains a mystery as to whether these children and their like were truly reared by wolves or whether, as it was asserted by the child psychologist Bruno Bettelheim, they were abandoned autistic children who had simply crawled into an animal's den.

its present apparently fanciful form? It is a strong possibility... and yet, like so many werewolf horror stories of its type, it is reported by many mythologists and historians, folklorists and psychologists as pure fact – James Stallybrass, for instance, in *Teutonic Mythology,* John Fiske in *Myths and Myth-makers,* and Walter E. Kelly in *Curiousities of Indo-European Tradition and Folk-lore.*

The origin of the werewolf superstition – the belief that a human being is capable of assuming an animal's form, most frequently that of a wolf – has never been satisfactorily explained.

Herodotus, the Greek historian who lived in the fifth century BC, says that the Greeks and the Scythians who settled on the shores of the Black Sea regarded the native Neurians as wizards, who were transformed into wolves for a few days of every year. He even speaks of a race of men who could change themselves at will into the shape of wolves and, when they desired, could just as easily resume their original form.

CRAVINGS FOR HUMAN FLESH

Centuries before the birth of Christ, the demon werewolf was looked upon as a human being possessed of an unnatural craving for human flesh who, by magical arts, had found a way to change at will into the form of a ravening wolf in order more readily to gratify this horrible appetite. Once transformed, the ancient sages believed, the werewolf possessed the very strength and cunning of the savage wolf-beast, though retaining his recognisably human voice and eyes.

The transformation of men into wolves is found in Roman literature also as a work of magic. Virgil, writing in the first century BC, is the first Latin poet to mention the superstition. Petronius, director of entertainment at Nero's court from AD 54 to 68, also tells a fine werewolf yarn in his satirical picaresque romance, the *Satyricon.*

The excessively hirsute – such as Jojo, right, dubbed the 'dog-faced boy' – have sometimes been thought to be werewolves, but erroneously so.

Elements of the werewolf legend passed into the story of Little Red Riding Hood, as shown in the illustration by Doré, below.

Certain Greek and Roman traditions represent the transformation of man into wolf as a punishment for sacrificing a human victim to a god. On such occasions, said Pliny (AD 62–113), the victim was taken to the edge of a lake and, having swum to the far shore, changed into a wolf. In this condition, he roamed the countryside with fellow wolves for a period of nine years. If, during this time, he abstained from eating human flesh, he resumed his original form, which would not have been exempt from the ravages of increased age.

Another mythological instance of shape-changing as a punishment for sin is recorded by Ovid (43 BC–AD 18) in his narrative poem *Metamorphoses*. In it, he recounts legends involving miraculous transformations of shape from the Creation to the time of Julius Caesar. He tells, for instance, how Lycaon, mythical King of Arcadia, presumed to test the omniscience of Jupiter by placing before him a dish of human flesh – for which crime he was immediately transformed into a wolf, to become for evermore a source of terror to his pastoral subjects.

The methods used to effect such transformations differed widely. Sometimes the change was spontaneous and uncontrollable; sometimes, as in the transformations described in Norse and Icelandic sagas, it was achieved simply by assuming the skin of a real wolf. But, in many cases, all that was needed was the use of a charm that, while involving no actual change in the human body, caused all onlookers to imagine that they really saw a wolf. Some transformed men claimed they could regain human form only by means of certain herbs, such as poisonous aconite or hemlock, or by rubbing ointments on their bodies.

WITCHES AND WEREWOLVES

So genuine was belief in such tales of transformation that, in the 15th and 16th centuries, werewolves throughout Europe were regarded in the same light as witches and wizards, and anyone suspected of being a werewolf was burnt or hanged with the utmost cruelty, especially in France and Germany. As Elton B. McNeil explains in *The Psychoses*, commenting on this era of flagellantism (self-injury), tarantism (dancing mania), mass hysteria, hypochondriacal delusion, projection or hallucination, and werewolfism:

'Attitudes reflected a psychology influenced by the belief that whom the gods will destroy, they first make mad. Madness, as an expression of the will of God, became epidemic. Its cure became a religious ritual designed to use the psychotic as a target for religious persecution and as a means of reaffirming the worth of the blessed, innocent, and pure. Blessed were those who exposed persons who had sold their souls to the Devil. The classic hunt of the witches was a side product in the search for salvation.'

The hunt for werewolves was a manifestation of much the same sort of religious feeling; indeed, witch trials and werewolf trials are clearly interrelated. But it is in witch-crazed France that the most numerous instances of werewolves are to be found. In one period of little over 100 years – between 1520 and 1630 – France could record a staggering 30,000 cases of werewolfism – a fact documented in the proceedings of werewolf trials that are preserved in the public records.

In 1573 at Dôle, near Dijon in central France, a werewolf named Gilles Garnier was accused of devastating the countryside and devouring little children and, after confessing to the crimes, was burnt at the stake.

A werewolf devours his victim, below, in an illustration from the former South African magazine Die Brandwag (The Fire-Watch).

The illustration, bottom, shows an 18th-century werewolf transformation. It was believed that, if the werewolf's clothes were hidden, he would be unable to resume human form.

Years later, in 1598, in a wild and desolate area near Caude, a group of French countrymen stumbled across the horribly mutilated, blood-spattered body of a 15-year-old boy. A pair of wolves, which had been devouring the corpse, ran off into a nearby thicket as the men approached. They gave chase – and almost immediately they found a half-naked man crouching in the bushes, sporting long hair and an unkempt beard and long, dirty claw-like nails, which were clotted with fresh blood and the shreds of human flesh.

The man, Jacques Rollet, was a pathetic, half-witted specimen under the curse of a cannibal appetite. He had been in the process of tearing to

In the 16th-century engraving, left, a wolf-headed Lycaon, mythical king of Arcadia, carries an axe to kill Jupiter, the supreme Roman god. Lycaon had presumed to test if Jupiter could distinguish between human and animal flesh, and was punished for his arrogance by being turned into a werewolf.

pieces the corpse of the boy when disturbed by the countrymen. Whether or not there were any wolves in the case, except those that excited imaginations may have conjured up, it is impossible to determine. But it is certain that Rollet supposed himself to be a wolf, and killed and ate several people under the influence of this delusion, a psychiatric condition known as *lycanthropy*. He was sentenced to death, but the law courts of Paris reversed the sentence and charitably shut him up in a madhouse – an institution where most suspected werewolves should probably have lived out their days rather than being executed.

DEVIL PACT

Another significant werewolf case occurred in the early 17th century. Jean Grenier was a boy of 13, partially idiotic and of strongly marked canine physiognomy – his jaws stuck forward, and his canine teeth showed under his upper lip. He believed himself to be a werewolf. One evening, meeting some young girls, he terrified them by saying that, as soon as the Sun had set, he would turn into a wolf and eat them for supper.

A few days later, one little girl, having gone out at nightfall to tend to the sheep, was attacked by some creature that in her terror she mistook for a wolf, but that afterwards proved to be none other than Jean Grenier. She beat him off with her sheep-staff, and fled home.

When brought before the law courts of Bordeaux, he confessed that, two years previously, he had met the Devil one night in the woods, had

signed a pact with him and received from him a wolfskin. Since then, he had roamed about as a wolf after dark, resuming his human shape by daylight. He had killed and eaten several children whom he had found alone in the fields, and once he had entered a house while the family were out and taken a baby from its cradle.

A careful investigation by the court proved that these statements were true, certainly as far as the cannibalism was concerned. There is little doubt that the missing children were eaten by Jean Grenier, and there is no doubt that the half-witted boy was firmly convinced that he was a wolf.

In more recent times, the werewolf phenomenon has retreated somewhat into the realms of fantasy, but has done so without losing any of its grim horror. Nevertheless, tales of real werewolves do crop up from time to time. Three werewolves were said to haunt the forested Ardennes area of Belgium just before the First World War, while in Scotland at about the same time a hermit shepherd in the area of Inverness was rumoured to be a werewolf. In 1925, a whole village near Strasbourg testified that a local boy was a werewolf; and, five years later, a French werewolf scare terrorised Bourg-la-Reine, just south of Paris, in an incident related by Pierre van Paasen in his book, *Days of Our Years.*

MURDEROUS BEAST

In more recent years, werewolf scares have also occurred the world over. In 1946, for instance, a Navajo Indian reservation was frequently plagued by a murderous beast that was widely reported as a werewolf. (Navajo traditions are rich in werewolf tales). Three years later, in Rome, a police patrol was sent to investigate the strange behaviour of a man suffering from werewolf delusions: he regularly lost control at the time of a full moon and let out loud and terrifying howls.

In Singapore, in 1957, police were again called to look into what the authorities believed was a long series of werewolf attacks on the residents of a particular nurses' hostel on the main island. One nurse awoke to find ' a horrible face, with hair reaching to the bridge of the nose,' and long protruding fangs, glaring down at her. The mystery was never solved, nor was the case of the 16-year-old schoolgirl at Rosario do Sul, in southern Brazil who, in 1978, suffered terrible 'evil visions and demons', and who believed she had been taken over by the spirit of a savage wolf

In 1975, Britain's newspapers were full of the most extraordinary reports about a 17-year-old youth from the village of Eccleshall, Staffordshire. In the awful belief that he was slowly turning into a werewolf, he terminated his mental agonies by plunging a flick-knife into his heart. One of his workmates told the inquest jury that the youth had made a frantic telephone call to him just before his death. 'He told me,' said the witness, 'that his face and hand were changing colour and that he was changing into a werewolf. He would go quiet and then start growling.'

The werewolf tradition may be built on ignorance and delusion, but its influence on the mind of the weak and sick has always been powerful and most probably will remain so.

BORLEY: A HAUNTING TALE

WAS BORLEY RECTORY REALLY 'THE MOST HAUNTED HOUSE IN ENGLAND' — OR WAS ITS FAME BASED ON A PUBLICITY STUNT BY GHOST-HUNTER HARRY PRICE? INDEED, WAS PRICE NO MORE THAN A HEADLINE-SEEKING FRAUD?

Borley parish church stands on a hillside overlooking the valley of the river Stour, which marks the boundary between the counties of Essex and Suffolk in England. Borley is hardly large enough to merit being called a village. The hundred or so inhabitants of this country parish, mainly agricultural workers and weekend cottagers, do their shopping and socialising in Long Melford or Sudbury, the two nearest small towns on the Suffolk side. For more important business, they must make the journey from Borley Green to Bury St Edmunds, a town that lies about 25 miles (40 kilometres) away.

Harry Price, the well-known ghost-hunter, psychical researcher and author, put the parish of Borley on the map when he wrote a book about the haunting of the rectory of the parish church, seen **below**.

But, in 1940, the publication of a book entitled *The Most Haunted House in England* suddenly made the community world-famous. Then, in 1946, a further volume, *The End of Borley Rectory,* set the seal on its fame. Both were written by the flamboyant ghost-hunter Harry Price, who put psychical research into the headlines in his day. The two books claimed that Borley Rectory, a gloomy Victorian house that had burned down in 1939, had been the focal point of some remarkably varied paranormal phenomena. These included a phantom coach, a headless monk, a ghostly nun (who may or may not have been the monk's lover), the spirit of a former vicar, eerie lights, water that turned into ink, mysterious bells, and a variety of 'things that went bump in the night'.

'One of the events of the year 1940' was how the first book was described by *Time and Tide* in its glowing review, while the *Church Times* said that it would 'remain among the most remarkable contributions ever made to the study of the paranormal'. Price, who professed to have devoted 10 years to his study of Borley's ghosts, continued to lecture,

broadcast and write on the subject until his death on 29 March 1948. An obituary in *The Times* the following day summed him up as a psychical researcher with 'a singularly honest and clear mind on a subject that by its very nature lends itself to all manner of trickery and chicanery'.

Not everyone who knew or worked with Price agreed with this glowing testimonial, however. Some months after his death, and with the danger of libel safely out of the way, an article by Charles Sutton of the *Daily Mail* appeared in the *Inky Way Annual*, a World's Press News publication. Writing of a visit he had paid to Borley with another colleague, in 1929, in the middle of Price's first investigation, Sutton said that he had discovered what might be fraud on Price's part. After a large pebble had hit Sutton on the head, he found that Price had bricks and pebbles in his pockets.

GRAVE SUSPICIONS

On a more careful investigation, two members of the Society for Psychical Research (SPR) – Lord Charles Hope and Major The Hon. Henry Douglas-Home – confessed that they had serious doubts about certain phenomena that they, too, had witnessed at the rectory in the late 1920s. Both of them filed testimony with the SPR, stating that they had grave suspicions. Douglas-Home went so far as to accuse Price of having a 'complete disregard for the truth in this matter'. He told how, on one occasion, he was accompanying Price around the rectory in the darkness when he heard a rustling that reminded him of cellophane being crumpled. Later, he sneaked a look into Price's suitcase and found a roll of cellophane with a torn edge.

It was as a result of this testimony that the Council of the SPR invited three of their members, Dr Eric J. Dingwall, Mrs K. M. Goldney and Mr Trevor H. Hall, to undertake a new survey of the evidence. They were given access to Price's private papers and correspondence by his literary executor, Dr Paul Tabori. They also had access to documents in the Harry Price Collection, which Price had placed on permanent loan with the University of London in 1938 and which was bequeathed to that institution on his death. This survey took five years to prepare

In the picture above, ghost-hunter Harry Price speaks on the radio direct from a haunted house in Meopham, Kent, in 1936. On a much publicised trip to Germany with C.E.M. Joad, below, Price is seen helping to recreate a magical scene on the Brocken in the Harz Mountains in 1932.

and was published in 1956 under the title *The Haunting of Borley Rectory*.

The reviews of this book were as enthusiastic as those of Price's two volumes in the 1940s, although for diametrically different reasons. The *Sunday Times* said that the Borley legend had been demolished 'with clinical thoroughness and aseptic objectivity'; while Professor A.G.N. Flew in the *Spectator* commented that the 'shattering and fascinating document' proved that Borley had been 'a house of cards built by the late Harry Price out of little more than a pack of lies'.

There, perhaps, the matter should have rested, but due to a combination of factors it did not. The principal reason may have been that Borley had made sensational copy for the world's popular newspapers for over a quarter of a century, and even the most objective of reporters dislikes seeing a good source of news dry up.

The media glossed over the painstaking evidence of Dingwall, Goldney and Hall. One account referred to them as 'the scoffers who accused Harry Price, the greatest of ghost-seekers, of rigging the whole legend'. And once more, the events described by Price were said to be 'puzzling, frightening, and inexplicable'. Peter Underwood, president of the Ghost Club, and the late Dr Tabori, returned to Price's defence in 1973 with a book entitled *The Ghosts of Borley: Annals of the Haunted Rectory*, dedicating it to 'the memory of Harry Price, the man who put Borley on the map'.

In his book *The Occult*, Colin Wilson made a fair and scrupulously unbiased summing up of the evidence for and against the Borley case. His conclusion was that 'a hundred other similar cases could be extracted [from SPR records]... Unless someone can produce a book proving that Price was a pathological liar with a craving for publicity, it is necessary to suspend judgement.'

Then, in 1978, SPR investigator Trevor H. Hall set out to prove Price 'a pathological liar with a craving for publicity'. The title of his book, *Search for Harry Price*, was a pun based on Price's own autobiography, *Search for Truth*.

Had it been less carefully documented, Hall's book could have been fairly described as a piece of muckraking. He revealed, for instance, that Price's father was a London grocer who had seduced and married Price's mother when she was 14 and he was over 40. Price himself, in his autobiography, had claimed to be the son of a wealthy paper manufacturer who came from 'an old Shropshire family'.

Price also stated that his childhood had been spent between the London stockbroker suburb of Brockley and the family's country home in Shropshire. He said that he usually 'broke his journey' there on the way to and from school, implying that he was educated at a boarding school. But Hall's researches clearly show the family home to have been in New Cross, far less salubrious than Brockley. Price, said Hall, attended a local secondary school, Haberdasher's Aske's Hatcham Boys' School, a perfectly respectable lower middle class establishment, not a boarding school. And the only connection with Shropshire was that Price's grandfather was landlord of the Bull's Head at Rodington.

Peter Underwood, above, was the president of the Ghost Club who came down on the side of Price in the controversy over his integrity.

The ruins of Borley Rectory, below, are as they appeared four years after the building was completely destroyed by a mysterious fire. This did not end the speculation over its haunting, however.

According to Price, he had held a directorship in his father's paper manufacturing company after leaving school, spending the 10 years between the end of his schooldays and his marriage in 1908 as an amateur coin collector and archaeologist. In fact, according to Hall, Price earned his living in New Cross in a variety of odd ways. He took photographs of local shopfronts for advertising purposes; hired out his portable gramophone and records for dances, parties and other functions; performed conjuring tricks at concerts – a skill that he was later accused of using during his Borley investigation; and peddled glue, paste and a cure for foot-rot in sheep from door to door in the Kent countryside. But Harry Price certainly had a flair for writing, as the impressive sales of his books – he wrote 17 in all – testify.

EXTRAVAGANT CLAIMS

In 1902, Price wrote an article for his old school magazine, *The Askean*, about the excavation of a Roman villa in Greenwich Park, quoting as his source a book written by the director of the project. But by 1942, in *Search for Truth*, he was claiming that he had actually helped to excavate the site. Price also contributed a series of articles to the *Kentish Chronicle* on coins and tokens of the county, following this up with another series for Shropshire's *Wellington Journal* on 'Shropshire tokens and mints'.

Hall asked the Reverend Charles Ellison, Archdeacon of Leeds and a leading authority on numismatics, to examine Price's writings on coins. The archdeacon found them to be straight plagiarisms from two obscure works on the subject. 'It is unsafe to rely on any statement made by Harry

she was a French woman called Marie Lairre. On the subject of this and subsequent seances he held, Sydney Glanville was almost apologetic to SPR researchers Dingwall, Goldney and Hall, admitting that suggestion had played a part: all three Glanvilles had studied the history of the Borley hauntings.

After the story of the nun's ghost had appeared in *The Most Haunted House in England*, Price received an elaborate theory from Dr W. J. Phythian-Adams, Canon of Carlisle, to the effect that Marie Lairre had been induced to leave her convent and marry one of the local landowners. She had been strangled by her husband and buried in a well on the site of the rectory. The canon also suggested that the ghost of the former nun stole a French dictionary from the residents of Borley Rectory in the 19th century so that she could brush up on her English in order to communicate with them.

Despite other preposterous twists in the canon's theory, Price seized on it eagerly; and Hall even accuses him of manufacturing and planting evidence to back it up. Part of this evidence was two French medals that Price claimed had appeared as 'apports' during his first visit to the rectory in 1929. One was a Roman Catholic confirmation medal and the other, a badge or pass issued to

Price which lacks independent confirmation,' he abruptly concluded.

Hall reported that Price's financial independence came from marriage to Constance Knight, who inherited a fortune from her father. It was her means – and not family wealth as Price claimed – that gave him the leisure to put his days of peddling behind him and embark on his career as psychical researcher and book collector. The assembling of a library of occult and magical books running into several thousand volumes was, said Hall, 'Price's most useful achievement during his life'.

Even the library seemed to offer opportunities for chicanery, however. In the collection, Hall found several valuable books clearly marked with the imprint of the SPR. Price had catalogued them as his own, even attaching his own book-plates.

Price's book-plates were a source of interest and amusement for Hall, as well as another example of Price's deviousness. Price used two crested plates. One featured a lion rampant, which proved on investigation to be the family crest of Sir Charles Rugge-Price of Richmond, with whom Harry Price had no connection. The other, bearing a crest and coat of arms, carried the name 'Robert Ditcher-Price' and the address 'Norton Manor, Radnor'. Hall's investigations revealed that the crest and arms were those of Parr, Lancashire, and that Norton Manor belonged to Sir Robert Green-Price, Baronet, whose family had lived there since the 17th century. A letter from Lady Jean Green-Price unequivocally stated that she had never heard of Robert Ditcher-Price and that she was 'quite certain that he never resided at Norton Manor'.

In his first book on Borley Rectory, Price used a version of a 'nun's tale' supplied by the Glanville family – father Sydney, son Roger and daughter Helen. While holding a seance with a planchette at their home, Helen Glanville elicited the information that a nun had been murdered at Borley and that

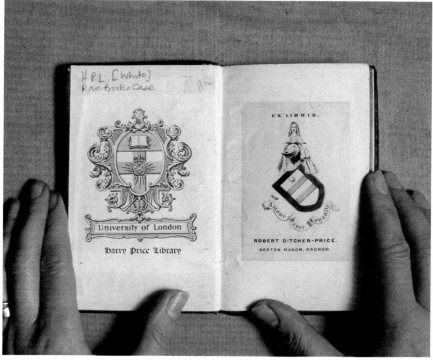

members of the National Assembly after the French Revolution. Yet, previously, Price had said that there was only one apported medal, as Price's faithful secretary confirmed.

PUZZLING FINDS

Hall also recounts how Price had excavated what he called a 'well' in the ruined cellars of Borley Rectory in 1943, discovering a human jawbone in the soft earth. The well turned out to be a modern concrete basin; and during the demolition of the ruins, a switch and lengths of wire were found in the cellar, though the house had never been supplied with electricity. In this account, there is an implicit suggestion that Price used this equipment to light the cellars as he secretly buried the jawbone for later discovery.

Price's accounts of psychical research projects are shown time and again to be inaccurate, almost entirely invented, or presented over the years in different versions with contradictory details. *Search for Harry Price* certainly fulfils Colin Wilson's criterion: it even shows Price as a confirmed liar and publicity-seeker. An absurd experiment in which Price and Professor C. E. M. Joad conducted a magical ceremony in the Harz Mountains in Germany for a regiment of press photographers certainly seems to prove the latter.

But does the tarnishing of Price's character necessarily mean that the haunting of Borley Rectory was fraudulent? From the year the rectory was built in 1863 until 1929, when Price first became interested in it, stories circulating in the area had seemed to suggest a succession of paranormal happenings at the site. Furthermore, from 1930 to 1937, Price visited Borley only once, and yet at least 2,000 allegedly paranormal incidents were recorded during that time. In a year straddling 1937 and 1938, when Price rented the empty rectory and recruited a team of independent witnesses through

Three of Harry Price's book-plates are shown above. The one on the far right, bearing the name of 'Robert Ditcher-Price' and the address 'Norton Manor, Radnor', was investigated by Hall.

an advertisement in *The Times* to live there with him, several incidents were reported even in Price's absence. And between Price's residency and 27 February 1939, when the rectory was 'mysteriously' destroyed by fire at midnight, several other extremely odd events occurred, as we shall see in the next part of this series.

> ❝ MORE DAMAGINGLY, PERHAPS, EYEWITNESSES CAME FORWARD TO TESTIFY THAT PRICE HAD DONE MORE THAN BIAS THE RESULTS… AND WHEN LIFE MAGAZINE PUBLISHED A PICTURE OF A BRICK APPARENTLY TELEPORTED INTO THE AIR AT BORLEY, WHY DID PRICE 'FORGET' THAT DEMOLITION WORK WAS IN PROGRESS AND THAT THE BRICK HAD ACTUALLY BEEN THROWN BY A LABOURER WHO WAS HIDDEN FROM THE CAMERA LENS? ❞
>
> JOHN FARLEY AND SIMON WELFARE, ARTHUR C. CLARKE'S WORLD OF STRANGE POWERS

LARGE, DARK AND UGLY, BORLEY RECTORY SEEMED TO INVITE HAUNTING. AND WITH THE ARRIVAL OF GHOST-HUNTER HARRY PRICE, IT BECAME A VERITABLE HIVE OF PARANORMAL ACTIVITY. BUT WAS SOMEONE PERHAPS HELPING THINGS ALONG?

Presented to The Rev. Henry Foyster Bull on his Marriage by the Choir and Organist of Borley Church. September 12. 1911

Although it served as rectory to the 12th-century Borley Church, which stood amid ancient gravestones on the opposite side of the Sudbury road, the 'most haunted house in England' was only 76 years old when it burned to the ground in the winter of 1939. It was an ugly, two-storey building of red brick, its grounds dotted with tall trees that cast gloom on many of its 23 rooms. The rectory had been built in 1863 by the Reverend Henry D. E. Bull, who was both a local landowner and rector of Borley Church, to house his wife and 14 children.

The Reverend Harry Bull – seen posing with the choir of Borley Church, above – like his father before him, perpetuated the story of the haunting of the rectory by a nun.

The gloomy 23-room rectory is seen, below, in a photograph taken from the tower of the church.

Immediately behind and to one side of the house lay a farmyard bounded by a cottage, stabling and farm buildings. When an extra wing was added to the house in 1875, a small central courtyard resulted. The dining-room fireplace was carved with figures of monks, a decoration suggesting that the Reverend Bull may have believed a local legend that a 13th-century monastery had once occupied the spot. It was one of the monks from this monastery who gave rise to the first ghost story about the site. This monk was said to have eloped with a nun from

BORLEY: THE TENSION MOUNTS

a convent at Bures, some 8 miles (13 kilometres) away. But the couple were caught and executed, he being beheaded, while she was walled up in the convent. Their ghosts were said to haunt the area. But the roots of this tale were cut away in 1938 by a letter from the Essex Archaeological Society to Sidney Glanville, one of the most diligent and honest volunteer investigators for ghost-hunter and author Harry Price. It stated that neither the monastery nor the nunnery had ever existed.

However, there is evidence that both the Reverend Henry Bull and his son and successor as rector, the Reverend Harry Bull, enjoyed telling the story. Indeed, it gained currency particularly among Sunday school children, many of whom presumably grew up believing it – in view of its source – to be 'gospel' in every respect.

Before this first 'nun's tale' was replaced by a later version, reports grew that various members of the Bull family – notably two of the sisters, Millie and Ethel – had seen a shadowy figure in the long rectory garden moving across what then became known as the 'nun's walk'. This route followed the path of an underground stream, along which clouds of gnats were inclined to drift on warm summer evenings. The two sisters told Price that they had seen the nun in July 1900, adding only that it was 'evening' and 'sunlit' – so no one can be sure it was not in fact a formation of gnats. A later rector, the Reverend G. Eric Smith, told of being startled by a 'white figure' that turned out to be the smoke from a bonfire; while V. C. Wall, a *Daily Mirror* reporter, saw a similar apparition that proved to be the maid.

The Bull family lived at Borley Rectory in basic discomfort – without gas, electricity or mains water – for almost 65 years. When his father died in 1892, Harry took over as rector and continued to live in

Harry Bull dozed away his last years in the summer-house, above. He claimed that he saw the ghostly nun and other apparitions while he rested here.

At the spot below, the ghost of the nun was said to disappear after her walk around the rectory garden.

the house with his numerous siblings. At least three of the family remained in occupation until Harry's death in June 1927, but he moved across the road to Borley Place when he married in 1911, returning to the rectory in 1920, presumably after his wife's death.

CURIOUS ACOUSTICS

Despite the architectural gloom of their surroundings, the younger Bulls seem to have been a lively crowd, according to the testimony of friends and acquaintances who contacted researchers in the late 1940s and early 1950s. The house had curious acoustics that lent themselves to practical jokes. According to Major the Hon. Henry Douglas-Home of the Society for Psychical Research, footsteps in the courtyard at the rear of the house and voices in the adjoining cottage could clearly be heard in the rectory, along with noise made by the hand pump in the stable yard. These provided plenty of thumps and groans, he said. Another source told researchers that the young Bull sisters took a delight in telling maids that the house was 'haunted'; and one old servant mentioned that, after being primed in this way by Edith Bull, she had heard 'shuffling' noises outside her room.

As he grew older, Harry Bull added his own contributions to the village gossip. He appears to have had narcolepsy, a condition in which the sufferer is always drowsy, and took to sleeping for most of the day in a summer-house. After his snoozes, he claimed he had seen the nun, had heard the phantom coach in which she had eloped with the monk, and had spoken to an old family retainer named Amos, who had been dead for years. By 1927, when Bull died and the family finally left the rectory, it had become a 'haunted house' in local imagination, and this reputation was probably enhanced as the house lay empty and dilapidated for over a year.

In October 1928, the new rector of Borley arrived. The Reverend G. Eric Smith had spent his early married life in India; but when his wife fell seriously ill there, he decided to return home, take holy orders, and seek a living. Desperation may have been setting in when he accepted Borley, for he took it on trust. He and his wife were dismayed when they discovered the rectory's condition.

To add to their troubles, during the first winter, the Smiths soon heard that the house was 'haunted'. The 'ghosts' themselves did not trouble them, however. As Mrs Smith was to write in a letter to the *Church Times,* neither of them thought the house haunted by anything but 'rats and local superstition'.

Smith's main worry was that the more nervous of his parishioners were unwilling to come to the rectory for evening meetings. So when he failed to talk them out of their fears, he took what was perhaps the fatal step of writing to the editor of the *Daily Mirror* to ask for the address of a psychical research society. He hoped that trained investigators could solve the mystery in a rational way and allay the fears of the locals.

Instead, the editor sent reporter, V. C. Wall; and on Monday, 10 June 1929, he filed the first sensational newspaper account about Borley Rectory. His story talked of 'ghostly figures of headless coachmen and a nun, an old-time coach, drawn by two bay horses, which appears and vanishes mysteriously, and dragging footsteps in empty rooms...'

The spectral nun and the phantom coach, believed to haunt the site of Borley Rectory, are illustrated below. In some versions of the story, the drivers of the coach were beheaded, which accounts for the headless figures in this picture.

The figure, bottom, *points out the place where the apparitional coach would vanish.*

The *Mirror* editor also telephoned Price, who made his first visit two days later. With Price's arrival, 'objective phenomena' began for the first time. Almost as soon as he set foot on the premises, a flying stone smashed a window, an ornament shattered in the hallway, and showers of apports – pebbles, coins, a medal and a slate – rattled down the main stairs. The servants' bells jangled of their own accord, and keys flew out of their locks. During a seance held in the Blue Room – a bedroom overlooking the garden with its 'nun's walk' – rappings on a wall mirror, supposedly made by the late Harry Bull, were heard by Price and his secretary, Wall, the Smiths, and two of the Bull sisters who were visiting the house.

Price made several trips to the house during the weeks that followed, and during each visit experienced strange phenomena that were duly reported in the *Daily Mirror* by Wall.

The results were predictable: far from quelling his parishioners' fears, the Reverend Smith had not only unwittingly increased them but added another dimension to his catalogue of woes, for the district

" AT BORLEY RECTORY, REPORTED PHENOMENA OVER A LONG PERIOD INCLUDED MATERIALIZATIONS OF THE NUN... BELL-RINGING, FOOTSTEPS, RAPS... DOOR-LOCKING AND UNLOCKING... FIRES AND SMOKE... A GLUEY SUBSTANCE, FACE-SLAPPING... THESE AND OTHER ACTIVITIES WERE REPORTED BY UPWARDS OF EIGHTY WITNESSES. "

PETER UNDERWOOD, EXORCISM!

became invaded by sightseers night and day. Coach parties were even organized by commercial companies and the Smiths soon found themselves virtually under siege. On 14 July, distressed by the ramshackle house and its unwelcome visitors, they moved to Long Melford; and Smith ran the parish from there before taking another living in Norfolk in April 1930.

Price must have been made uneasy on at least two occasions at Borley. One of these was when some coins and a Roman Catholic medallion, featuring St Ignatius Loyola, 'materialised' and fell to the ground at about the same time as some sugar lumps flew through the air. When they were picked up, they were, recalled Mrs Smith, strangely warm to the touch, as if from a human hand. Her maid, Mary Pearson, a known prankster, gave her the solution: 'That man threw that coin,' she explained, 'so I threw some sugar.' An even more farcical incident marked the second near-miss for Price during a further seance in the Blue Room. Heavy footsteps were heard outside, accompanied by the slow rumble of shutters being drawn back. In the doubtless stunned hush that followed, Price asked aloud if it were the spirit of the Reverend Harry Bull. A guttural voice, clearly recognizable as that of a local handyman, replied: 'He's dead, and you're daft.'

Rats, Mrs Smith later averred, lay behind the bell ringing – the bell wires ran along rafters under the roof. As for a mysterious light that 'appeared' in an upstairs window, it was well-known locally as a trick reflection of light from the railway carriages that passed along the valley.

For six months after the Smiths left Borley parish, the rectory was unoccupied once more. Then, on 16 October 1930, the Reverend Harry Bull's cousin, Lionel A. Foyster, moved in as the new rector. The Reverend Foyster, a man in his early fifties, had moved back home from his previous post as rector of Sackville, Nova Scotia, which he had held between 1928 and 1930. He suffered

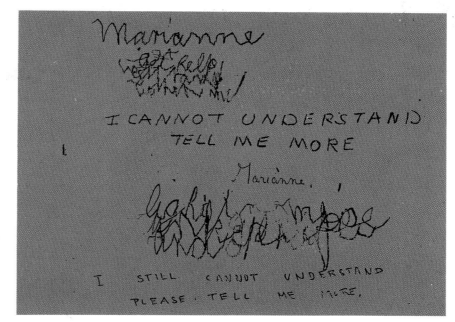

Paranormal phenomena increased when the Foysters came to live at Borley Rectory, and included the spirit writing, top.

Investigation of the Borley haunting is one of the most controversial aspects of the career of Harry Price, seen above in his laboratory.

All manner of apports – including coins and pebbles – arrived at the foot of the main stairs of the rectory, left, soon after Harry Price's arrival.

from rheumatism but, despite this painful illness, he was a kindly and well-liked man. He was also deeply devoted to his attractive wife Marianne, some 20 years his junior, and their adopted daughter Adelaide, a child of about two-and-a-half.

During the five years that the Foysters lived at Borley, an estimated 2,000 'incidents' occurred, most of them within a period of about 14 months. These included voices, footsteps, objects being thrown, apparitions and messages scribbled in pencil on walls. It is probably true to say that, with one possible exception, none of these could be attributed to Harry Price, who visited the rectory only once while the Foysters were there. The day after his visit, on 15 October 1931, he wrote one of the few straightforward statements he was ever to make on the Borley mystery in a letter to a colleague: 'Although psychologically, the case is of great value, psychically speaking there is nothing in it.'

Six months had elapsed since the Smiths' departure and the Foysters' arrival, and in that time Borley Rectory had become more dilapidated than ever. According to her husband's cousins, the Bulls, Mrs Foyster hated the place from the moment she saw it. She made no friends locally, and her only companion, apart from Lionel, was a family friend, François D'Arles, a French-Canadian who was much nearer her own age. He rented the cottage at the rear of the house, and investigators from the Society for Psychical Research got the impression that he dominated the household. By 1932, Marianne Foyster and D'Arles had opened a flower shop together in London and returned to Borley only at weekends, the implication being that they had become lovers. Mrs Foyster often behaved oddly, if not hysterically, fainting when frustrated. Once she flung herself on her knees before assembled investigators to pray to St Anthony for 'vindication' when no manifestations were forthcoming – as though she expected to be able to produce them. And when the 'hauntings' of Borley Rectory began again shortly after the Foysters' arrival, villagers went so far as to accuse Marianne Foyster – to her face – of being behind them.

In 1878, a young woman named Esther Cox suddenly became the centre of 'mysterious manifestations' at her sister's home in Amherst, Nova Scotia. Esther saw apparitions visible to no one else. Objects were thrown, furniture was upset, small fires broke out in the house, and messages addressed to the girl were found scribbled on the walls. The 'hauntings' subsequently became the subject of a book, *The Haunted House: A True Ghost Story . . . The Great Amherst Mystery* by Walter Hubbell. It was a huge success, running through 10 editions and selling over 55,000 copies. But, in 1919, the American Society for Psychical Research printed a critical study by Dr Walter F. Prince, suggesting that the Amherst case was not in fact a poltergeist manifestation. It was, he said,

Hauntings at Borley Rectory, above, seemed to reach a peak when Marianne Foyster lived there. But it is still an open question as to whether she created the events herself.

The cottage, below, was once part of the Borley Rectory property and the home of François D'Arles.

trickery on the part of Esther Cox while in a state of dissociation, or conversion hysteria.

The township of Amherst is about 5 miles (8 kilometres) from the equally small community of Sackville, where another of Esther Cox's married sisters resided and where, 50 years afterwards, the Reverend Lionel Foyster and his wife Marianne lived. The Foysters would certainly have heard of the Amherst case; and the fact that Foyster used the pseudonym 'Teed' – the married name of Esther Cox's sister – when writing of the happenings at Borley Rectory during his stay there offers what is tantamount to proof that he not only knew

BORLEY REVISITED

of the Amherst case but was familiar with its details. It seems likely, therefore, that his wife also knew of the case, though whether she made deliberate – if unconscious – use of it for her own behaviour is a matter for conjecture.

The resemblance between both cases is indeed striking; and Dingwall, Goldney and Hall, in *The Haunting of Borley Rectory*, offer no less than 19 points of general concurrence, including the ringing of bells, throwing of objects, setting of small fires, and mysterious messages written on walls.

Shortly after Marianne Foyster arrived at Borley and took such an instant dislike to the place, she began to see 'apparitions'; but no one else did. Then the manifestations, so similar to the Amherst case, began. Her husband, loyal and devoted, answered villagers, who accused her of faking, that *he* could not see the visions because 'he wasn't psychic'; and, in her 'defence', he began to keep a rough record of events. This was not perhaps as helpful as he hoped it might be because, as he admitted, much of it was written later.

Ghost-hunter Harry Price, left, and Mrs K. M Goldney of the Society for Psychical Research, right, pose below with the Foyster family at Borley Rectory. The Foysters' adopted child Adelaide and an unidentified playmate complete the group portrait.

One of several messages that appeared on the walls of the rectory is reproduced, bottom. All of them were scribbled in pencil in a childish hand, and most were addressed to Marianne Foyster.

In October 1931, in answer to a plea from the Bull sisters, Harry Price returned to Borley once more. It is interesting to speculate on the motives behind the Bulls' concern: perhaps because they knew the source of the pranks and hoaxes during their own tenancy, they suspected the genuineness of the new 'haunting'. The same might be said of Harry Price, for he returned from his visit convinced that Mrs Foyster was directly responsible for fraud.

In their examination of the alleged phenomena, Dingwall, Goldney and Hall analyzed the incidents described in Foyster's first record, which he later elaborated upon. Treating the constant bell ringing as a single phenomenon, they isolated 103 different instances. Of these, 99 depended totally on Mrs Foyster's sincerity, three were readily attributable to natural causes, and only one was in any way 'inexplicable'.

Among the most suspicious incidents was the appearance of pencilled writings on the walls. Some seven messages appeared during the Foysters' tenancy, most of them addressed to Marianne and

"WHAT SEEMS CLEAR FROM ALL ACCOUNTS OF THE PLACE IS THAT THE GROUND ITSELF IS HAUNTED, AND CONTINUES TO BE SO... BORLEY IS A PLACE OF POWER, THE KIND OF PLACE THAT WOULD BE CHOSEN FOR A MONASTERY, AND THAT PROBABLY HELD SOME PAGAN SITE OF WORSHIP LONG BEFORE THAT."

COLIN WILSON, POLTERGEIST!

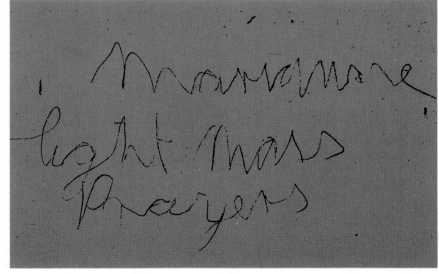

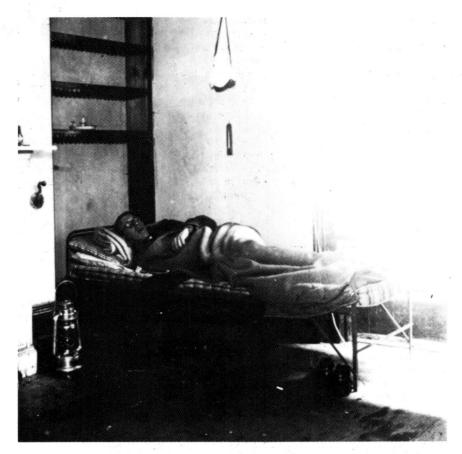

appealing for 'light, mass, prayers'. Another, not noted by Price in his Borley books, spelled 'Adelaide', the name of the Foysters' adopted daughter. All the messages were in a childish scribble. It has been speculated that little Adelaide may even have been responsible for one or both of the mysterious small fires that broke out in the rectory, for she was caught on at least one occasion trying to set fire to bedclothes.

In 1933, when the Foysters went on leave for six months, they left Canon H. Lawton as locum. Nothing untoward happened, though the canon – like Major Douglas-Home of the Society for Psychical Research – noted the curious acoustics of the house and surroundings. In any case, by then, Mrs Foyster was spending most of her time in London with François D'Arles at their flower shop. An exorcism by a group of Spiritualists the previous year, when Marianne and François first left to open their shop, seemed to have got rid of what the Foysters cosily called 'the goblins'. Or was it that Marianne Foyster was no longer on the premises?

In October 1935, the Foysters left Borley. When the Reverend A.C. Henning was appointed five months later, he chose to live elsewhere; and since this time, the rectors of Borley have lived at Liston or Foxearth rectories, parishes amalgamated with Borley since the 1930s.

But the battered, drama-ridden old house had still another four years of life to run. On 19 May 1937, Harry Price rented the rectory, and a week later inserted an advertisement in *The Times* asking for 'responsible persons of leisure and intelligence, intrepid, critical and unbiased' to form a rota of observers at the house. If, he later stated, they

One of Price's 48 volunteer investigators takes a break from his duties at the rectory, above. Price rented Borley for a year and gathered a team of observers through an advertisement in **The Times** *to work with him there. He did not ask for experience in psychical research but required his volunteers to have 'leisure and intelligence' and to be critical and unbiased.*

'knew nothing about psychical research, so much the better'.

Whether or not Harry Price and Marianne Foyster had used fraud for their own personal ends, a trickster who came on the scene in November 1938 was working for purely financial gain. He was Captain William Hart Gregson, who bought Borley Rectory six months after Price's tenancy expired. He immediately asked Price's advice about organizing coach trips to see his new property and broadcast on the radio, recounting several minor 'phenomena'. But his coach tour plans were brought to an abrupt end at midnight on 27 February 1939 when fire gutted the building, leaving only a few walls, charred beams and chimney stacks.

Sidney Glanville, one of Price's volunteer researchers and of impeccable reputation, said that, at a seance held at the Glanville home, an entity named 'Sunex Amures' had threatened to burn down Borley Rectory. But the real cause of the destruction of Borley Rectory was flatly stated by Sir William Crocker in his autobiography *Far from Humdrum: a Lawyer's Life*. Crocker, a distinguished barrister, and Colonel Cuthbert Buckle, an insurance adjuster, were both set the task of investigating the claim made by Gregson on behalf of the insurers. Crocker states: 'We repudiated his impudent claim for "accidental loss by fire"... pleading that he had fired the place himself.'

HOCUS POCUS

The ruins of Borley Rectory were finally demolished in the spring of 1944 and the site levelled. An orchard and three modern bungalows now occupy the spot. During the demolition, Price took a *Life* magazine photographer and researcher, Cynthia Ledsham, to Borley; and by sheer fluke, the photographer captured on film a brick that was apparently 'levitated' by unseen forces but was in fact thrown by a worker. *Life* published the photograph over a jokey caption; but Price, in his book *The End of Borley Rectory*, claimed it as a final 'phenomenon'. Cynthia Ledsham was astounded, calling it 'the most bare-faced hocus pocus on the part of... Harry Price.'

The truth is that the haunting of Borley Rectory was the most bare-faced hocus pocus from start to finish, with Price feeding his craving for personal publicity from it in the most short-sighted way. For, as was shown after his death, his shallow frauds could not hope to withstand investigation.

In a letter to C.G. Glover in 1938, Price wrote: 'As regards your various criticisms, the alleged haunting of the rectory stands or falls not by the reports of our recent observers, but by the extraordinary happenings there of the last 50 years.'

But Harry Price was to write to Dr Dingwall in 1946 in reference to the occasion when a glass of water was 'changed' into ink: 'I agree that Mrs Foyster's wine [*sic*] trick was rather crude, but if you cut out the Foysters, the Bulls, the Smiths, etc., something still remains.'

One great irony certainly remains. Despite the demolition of Price's pack of lies, ghost-hunters of the 1960s and 1970s doggedly persisted in investigating the area. And they may finally just have stumbled on something truly paranormal – not at the rectory site, but in Borley Church itself.

IF SPECTRAL FIGURES APPEAR ON A PHOTOGRAPH WHEN NOTHING OF THE KIND WAS VISIBLE AT THE TIME THEY WERE TAKEN, PSYCHIC INVESTIGATION IS CLEARLY CALLED FOR. WHO ARE THESE GHOSTLY 'EXTRAS'?

The ease with which 'extras' may be imposed upon photographs has led most people to believe that many, if not all spirit photographs are in some way fraudulent. However, while the greater number of so-called psychic pictures are indeed intended to amuse or defraud, a few have been made in circumstances that place them on a level beyond ordinary understanding.

The most extraordinary spirit photographs of all have been made during seances, often under rigid test conditions; but a few interesting ones have also been made unexpectedly, and by amateurs. Someone takes a snapshot of a friend, of an interior, or of a pet, and afterwards finds, to his astonishment, the image of a face or figure – sometimes recognisably that of a deceased relative or friend. This occurs rarely, but it does happen; and many examples with written accounts have been preserved by archivists and librarians interested in

In the spirit photograph, below, taken by a certain Mrs Wickstead in 1928, an embracing couple – not seen by the photographer at the time – appear in the churchyard. The 'spirits' were not identified; and the Society for Psychical Research, who investigated the matter, could not explain them.

psychic phenomena. The earliest preserved examples of spirit photographs were of this order: they were taken by amateur photographers who had no specialist interest in psychic effects and who were disappointed at their portraits and landscapes being spoiled by the mysterious 'extras'.

It is generally accepted that spirit photography as such began in Boston, Massachusetts, USA, on 5 October 1861, when William Mumler accidentally produced his first spirit picture. But this date may not be entirely accurate. For, according to an early pioneer of Spiritualism in Boston, Dr H.F. Gardner, a few portraits exhibiting a second figure that could not be accounted for had been made previously at nearby Roxbury. The Roxbury photographer was an orthodox Christian who, after hearing about Mumler's pictures, refused to print any negatives containing 'spirits' on the grounds that, if these pictures had anything to do with Spiritualism, they were the work of the Devil.

The fact is that, well over a century later, we still do not know what causes 'spirits' to appear on prints. The majority of psychical researchers involved with spirit photography claim it occurs by the direct intervention of the spirits themselves. If one accepts such a theory, the phenomena may be viewed not so much as 'spirit photography', as 'photography by spirits'.

UNEXPECTED DEVELOPMENTS

The famous English journalist W.T. Stead was an early champion of spirit photography, and many portraits of him show images of recognised 'extras' alongside. After he died in the *Titanic* disaster in April 1912, he continued to converse from the spirit world with his daughter, Estelle, as she reported. And then the matter went further, for his image began to appear as an 'extra' alongside her in pictures. When Estelle asked him to say something about the actual production of such images, Stead insisted that the spirits were themselves involved with them – in order to convince us of the reality of life after death.

The spirit photographs made by professionals and participants in seances are fascinating enough. But it is the innocence and the element of the unexpected that permeate the accidental spirit photographs of amateurs that intrigue the investigator of the genre most.

One such example is a photograph taken in 1964 inside the English church of St Mary the Virgin, in Woodford, Northamptonshire. It was taken by 16-year-old Gordon Carroll who, with a friend, had been on a cycling tour. They had decided to visit the church because of its historic value – it is mentioned in the *Domesday Book*. After checking that the church was empty, Gordon took two pictures of the interior – one looking towards the altar, and another photograph of the rear of the interior.

The spirit of William T. Stead, who had died in the Titanic *disaster, appears, above, in a photograph of his living daughter Estelle. When she asked him how psychic photography came about, he replied that the spirits themselves were involved in producing the unexpected images.*

Arrows, above right, point to the ghostly heads of two drowned sailors, photographed by a passenger on the vessel, Watertown. The spectres had been seen in the waves for several days after the drowning, and the photographer deliberately took the picture to record this psychic phenomenon.

*In*Focus

NEGATIVE FINDINGS

The faking of spirit photographs seems to have begun almost as soon as the genuine product appeared in the mid-19th century. One of the most common faking techniques was the double exposure – not a problem with the large plates then in use. But a more cunning method involved the painting of a background screen with a special chemical, invisible to ordinary sight, which would show up on photographic film. This screen was pre-painted and placed behind the sitter. Other complex techniques were also devised by unscrupulous photographers.

The case now known as the 'Moss photographic fiasco' is among the most interesting of the proven frauds. During the early 1920s, G.H. Moss was employed as a chauffeur by a man who was interested in the paranormal. Moss was an amateur photographer, and one day brought a print with a ghostly 'extra' to his employer. The employer showed interest and, after some experiments on his own, introduced Moss to the British College of Psychic Science. Around 1924, Moss was given a year's contract to work under test conditions at the college, on a fixed salary. His work there was impressive and well-received – until, that is, he was exposed as a fraud.

Moss produced a number of spirit images that were recognised as the likenesses of dead relatives and friends by sitters. In one of these, shown *below*, the sitter was a trance medium. She recognised the 'extra' as her dead sister. A cut-out photograph of that sister was mounted alongside the 'extra' to illustrate the resemblance. In another, *right*, the image was recognised by a person observing the photographic session, though it was not clear whether the recognised individual was dead or alive.

A third example of Moss's work, *far right*, was made in a seance with the well-known medium Mrs Osborne Leonard on 5 January 1925. The sitter was informed by 'a voice from beyond' that he would be sitting for a photograph in eight days. The invisible speaker promised that she would reveal herself then.

After the pictures had been processed, the young photographer filed them away and only took them out a year later in preparation for a Christmas slide show. On examining the pictures, he and his friend saw that one of them featured a ghostly figure, apparently kneeling in front of the altar: its head was not visible since it was bowed down as if in prayer. The figure appeared to be wearing a monk's robes. Both Gordon and his friend at the time were convinced there had been no one at the altar when the photograph was taken, nor – according to a film processing expert – had any fraud been involved.

SPECTRAL PORTRAITS

Only rarely do amateur photographers take pictures in the knowledge that they are recording psychic phenomena. One of the few exceptions is the case of the *Watertown* pictures, which contain images of drowned seamen. These were deliberately taken by one of the passengers on board a vessel, the *Watertown,* from which two seamen had been swept overboard and drowned during the course of the journey. For several days afterwards, passengers and crew alike insisted that the seamen's spectral heads could be seen in the waves and spray.

Much more typical is the account of the curious extras on a snapshot taken by a certain Mrs Wickstead in 1928. The snapshot – now quite faded but never of first-rate quality – was one of two taken at the church in the village of Hollybush, not far from Hereford. Mrs Wickstead was on a car tour with friends and had stopped to see the church. She decided to take a photograph of her friend, Mrs Laurie, who in the event can barely be seen in the photograph. After the picture had been taken, Mrs Laurie drew Mrs Wickstead's attention to the grave of a soldier who had died on active service. Alongside this grave was another of a girl who had died shortly afterwards.

'I wonder if they were lovers?' Mrs Laurie had remarked to her companion.

In a letter to Sir Oliver Lodge, later President of the Society for Psychical Research (SPR), Mrs Wickstead wrote that Mrs Laurie had seemed impressed by the two graves and had made a point of showing them to her husband. 'We thought no more about it until about six weeks later when the film was developed and came out as you see, with these two figures on the path in the shadow of the yew tree,' Mrs Wickstead wrote. The two figures were in an embrace. The picture was investigated by the SPR, but the mystery of the 'extras' was never solved.

There have also been cases of sensitives both seeing and photographing spirits that have remained invisible to others present – but these are

That sitting, which had already been arranged without Mrs Leonard's knowledge, did indeed produce an 'extra' – and some of the sitter's friends insisted that the image bore a strong likeness to his recently deceased wife. A portrait of her was then pasted alongside so that a comparison could be made.

Moss was finally unmasked by the astute F. Barlow, at that time the Honorary Secretary for the now defunct Society for the Study of Supernormal Pictures. While Barlow was examining a group of Moss's negatives containing 'extras', he noticed a peculiar roughness on the edges of certain plates.

Closer examination showed that each negative bearing a spirit image had one edge that was filed. Detailed examination of the plate wrappings revealed that they had been skilfully opened by steaming and subsequently resealed.

Moss vehemently denied fraud and even signed a statement declaring his innocence. However, when faced with the filed plates, he made a confession. He had secretly opened certain plates and superimposed an image on them, marking them for later use by filing the edges.

" AMATEUR PHOTOGRAPHERS,
PRESS PHOTOGRAPHERS,
PROFESSIONAL PORTRAIT
PHOTOGRAPHERS, PSYCHIC
HEALERS, SPIRITUALIST MEDIUMS
AND PEOPLE WITH NO INTEREST
IN EITHER PHOTOGRAPHY OR
PSYCHIC MATTERS HAVE ALL
TAKEN PSYCHIC OR SUPERNORMAL
PHOTOGRAPHS AT ONE TIME
OR ANOTHER. "

CYRIL PERMUTT,

PHOTOGRAPHING THE SPIRIT

WORLD

rare. One of the most famous examples has become known as the 'Weston' photograph.

The Reverend Charles Tweedale and his family lived in Weston vicarage, a much haunted house in the town of Otley in West Yorkshire. While having lunch on 20 December 1915, Mrs Margaret Tweedale saw the apparition of a bearded man to the left of her son. The others around the table could see nothing. However, Margaret's husband immediately fetched the camera and took a picture of the area indicated by his wife. When the negative was developed, a portrait of the apparition appeared on the print.

SPIRITUAL INSTRUCTION

An extraordinary picture session that took place in Belgium seems to support the belief that the spirits intervene directly in psychic photography. In this instance, a spirit actually instructed an amateur photographer in the most precise manner as to how and when to take a picture in which the spirit would manifest itself. The picture was taken by Emile le Roux in 1909 and is one of the very few stereoscopic spirit photographs.

The instructions apparently came from a spirit who claimed to be the uncle of le Roux's wife. The spirit made contact through her while she was practising automatic writing in le Roux's presence. Through the automatic script, the 'uncle' said that he could be photographed at a later point in the day and gave instructions as to the time and necessary exposure. Le Roux, a keen amateur photographer, considered the exposure to be far too long; but he followed instructions and took the picture with his stereoscopic camera at the time indicated. The image of the deceased uncle not only appeared, but was quite recognisable. In its day, the plate became very famous – but time after time, le Roux had to defend himself against the usual charges of fraud.

*The spirit of a dead child appears, above left, **with her father on a portrait taken by a clairvoyant. Apparently, the girl was seen by the photographer when he took the picture, though she was not visible to others present.***

*The stereoscopic picture, above, **shows Madame le Roux practising automatic writing, while the spirit image of her uncle appears beside her face, to the left. Through the writing, the spirit gave the photographer instructions on how the picture shoud be taken.***

*The unidentified 'extra' on the print, left, **was photographed in Gloucester Cathedral around 1910.***

*The picture of a bottle, above right, **was allegedly made by the direct transfer of a thought on to a photographic plate in France in 1896, by a certain Commandant Darget.***

*The ghost of a woman, dead a week, is seen, right, **in a picture taken by her daughter. She is apparently sitting in the back seat. Experts said the photograph had not been tampered with.***

His own simple words echo the recurrent story of the amateur caught up in a mysterious process:

'In reality, this photograph was made under the most simple circumstances, and I would say that except for the strangeness of the spirit head, there were so few difficulties both before and after its execution that, in spite of the scepticism which arose within me and which has not yet quite vanished, I am forced to admit that in order to explain this negative, it is necessary to look in another direction than fraud or the double exposure of the plate.'

The subject of spirit photography greatly excited psychical investigators in the 1870s and 1880s, but no organised and sustained study seems to have been made. There are many references to the phenomenon in the *British Journal of Photography,* and a number of articles in the *Journal* of the SPR. But the issue was clouded by the controversy over Spiritualism, and no undistorted and full treatment of psychic photography itself has come down to us.

In any event, psychic photography did not end with the unexplained appearance of spirit forms on prints. One new form that has emerged in recent times is the manifestation of UFOs. What is more, since the main question is whether images on film can be produced without optical processes, thoughtography is of relevance too.

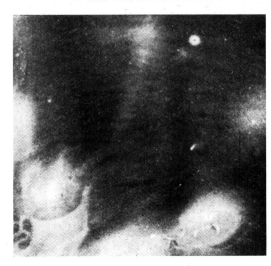

The term 'thoughtography' first came into use in Japan in 1910, following a series of tests by Tomokichi Fukurai of a clairvoyant who accidentally imprinted a calligraphic character on a photographic plate by psychic means. Later, the sensitive found he was able to do this by concentrated effort. Fukurai's work was published in English 20 years later, and experiments similar to his were then undertaken in Europe and the United States. But it was not until 1962 that interest in thoughtography was activated by Pauline Oehler, of the Illinois Society for Psychic Research, through her work with the American psychic Ted Serios.

Serios was much investigated under strictly controlled conditions, particularly by Dr Jule Eisenbud, a psychical researcher working mainly in Denver, Colorado, USA. In many experiments planned by Eisenbud over a period of two years, Serios could produce, at will, pictures of what he was thinking about – an old hotel, cars, a corner of a room, and many other mental images. He could also produce an image of a target set by himself or others. For example, one day he glanced casually at a travel magazine in Eisenbud's waiting room. The next day, he decided to produce a picture of London's Westminster Abbey, which he had noticed in the publication – and succeeded in doing so.

Thoughtography has continued to be subjected to psychical research; and although Ted Serios' ability to transfer his thoughts on to film has never been fully explained, neither has it ever been proved to be fraudulent.

Among the professional spirit photographers of the late 19th century, however, there were undoubtedly frauds – and a number of them were eventually exposed. But that, of course, does not negate the important fact that many 'spirit' images may well have been produced by paranormal means: indeed, it could still be the case today.

THE CURSE OF FYVIE CASTLE

AN ANCIENT CURSE LAID ON FYVIE CASTLE IN SCOTLAND IS SAID STILL TO BE EFFECTIVE TODAY. IS THERE TRUTH BEHIND THIS MACABRE LEGEND OF A MELANCHOLY GHOST?

Alexander Forbes-Leith bought Fyvie Castle in 1889. With it, he acquired both a curse and, perhaps, the only ghost that has ever signed its name in stone for later generations to see.

The castle, which stands some 30 miles (50 kilometres) north-west of Aberdeen, has been described as the 'crowning glory of Scottish baronial architecture'. Its foundations were laid before the Norman Conquest in 1066 and, since the 14th century, it has been held by only five great families.

Like many a blight on old Scottish families, the 'Fyvie curse' was the work of the ubiquitous Thomas the Rhymer. Although he was shrouded in legend and superstition, it seems certain that Thomas of Erceldoune was a real person. He was born in 1220 and is mentioned as witness to a deed at the Abbey of Melrose around 1240. In Peter of Langtoft's early 14th-century *Chronicle*, it is also stated that he was a poet.

In his own day, Thomas the Rhymer was widely credited as being the lover of the 'Queen of Elfland'. It was she who had given him the power of prophecy; and when he vanished, it was presumed that she had carried him off. It is more likely, however, that he entered a monastery or, as Sir Walter Scott believed, was murdered by robbers.

While he was alive, his travels were well-recorded both in local lore and in contemporary

The magnificent south front of Scotland's Fyvie Castle, above, *was extensively rebuilt in the early 16th century by Alexander Seton, Lord Fyvie,* right. *According to legend, three 'weeping stones' of ill omen had been built into the earlier fabric of Fyvie Castle: as long as they remained there, no heir would be born within the castle's walls.*

documents. But he cannot have been a welcome guest, since his prophecies invariably foretold disaster; bloodshed and general mayhem were his stock-in-trade. Nevertheless, few of the lairds visited by Thomas the Rhymer cared to turn him away in case even worse befell them. According to James Murray, the 19th-century editor of the five ancient manuscripts that tell Thomas' story, the gates of

Fyvie Castle had stood 'wall-wide' – that is, open for seven years and a day, awaiting his inevitable arrival. When he finally turned up, it was in a typically ostentatious style. 'He suddenly appeared before the fair building, accompanied by a violent storm of wind and rain, which stripped the surrounding trees of their leaves and shut the Castle gates with a loud crash. But while the tempest was raging on all sides, it was observed that, close to the spot where the Tammas [Thomas] stood, there was not wind enough to shake a pile of grass or a hair of his beard.' Not surprisingly, Thomas was far from pleased that the Castle gates should have slammed shut in his face. Angrily, he uttered the following blood-curdling prophecy:

> 'Fyvie, Fyvie, thou's never thrive
> As lang's there's in thee stanis [stones] three.
> There's ane intill [one in] the oldest tower,
> There's ane intill the ladye's bower,
> There's ane intill the water-yett [water gate]
> And thir three stanes ye's never get.'

This somewhat obscure pronouncement was taken to mean that three stones, known collectively as the 'weeping stones', which had originally been taken from a nearby church property, would act as evil omens to Fyvie Castle as long as they remained part of the building. Only one of the stones, the one originally in 'the ladye's bower', has been found as yet, and so the curse remains.

Today, this stone stands in a wooden bowl in the charter room. At times, it is bone dry, and at

The Seton Tower, above right, over the main gate, was being rebuilt by Lord Fyvie when he married his second wife in 1601. Because the new apartments in it were not ready for occupation, the couple spent their wedding night in a room in the older part of Fyvie Castle.

The panelled charter room, above, decorated with crescents, cinquefoils and the arms of the Seton family, was another of Lord Fyvie's improvements to the castle. The only one of the three 'weeping stones' that has been located is reputedly kept in a wooden bowl in this room.

others is seen to be 'exuding sufficient water to fill the bowl'. The stone said to be beneath the 'water-yett' has never been located; and the third one may have been built into what is now the Preston Tower since once, records an ancient document at the castle, 'when the rightful but dispossessed heir to the property approached, the water gushed forth in mournful salutation.'

Although Thomas the Rhymer was far from specific, the actual nature of the curse was interpreted as meaning that no heir would ever be born in the castle, and this is said to have been true since 1433. Furthermore, the castle would never pass from a father to his eldest son. This claim has held good. Indeed, among the Forbes-Leith family,

the last private owners of the castle, no first-born survived to inherit it. Perhaps none ever will; since 1984, Fyvie Castle has been in the hands of the National Trust for Scotland.

But there is another mystery surrounding Fyvie Castle. It, too, concerns a stone, and one that is situated immediately above the charter room. It forms a window-sill three storeys up the sheer face of the castle wall. The puzzle, which dates from the night of 27 October 1601, has so far defied any rational explanation. At that time, the laird was Alexander Seton, Lord Fyvie, afterwards first Earl of Dunfermline, and Lord President of the Scottish sessions.

In 1592, Seton married Dame Lilias (or Lilies) Drummond, daughter of Lord Patrick Drummond, another peer connected with the ruling house of Stuart. Dame Lilias was a handsome, happy woman, and for nine years she and her husband were contented together. In that time, she bore five daughters, four of whom survived to marry influential noblemen. However, Lilias was not as strong as her appearance suggested; and on 8 May 1601, she died at her husband's house in Fife, where she was buried.

On the stone window-sill, **left**, the name of Lord Fyvie's first wife, **D. LILIES DRUMMOND, has been carved upside down in characters nearly 3 inches (7 centimetres) high. The room, called the Drummond Room, is said to be the one occupied by Lord Fyvie and his second wife on their wedding night in 1601. During the night, they heard deep sighs; and in the morning, they discovered Dame Lilias' name incised outside the window.**

Dame Lilias was not quite 30 when she died. According to the historical record, Seton seems to have mourned her death, and the fact that he remained on good terms with his brother-in-law bears this out. Tradition, on the other hand, asserts something different: tired of waiting for the son and heir who never came, Seton had begun an affair with the beautiful Lady Grizel Leslie, daughter of the Master of Rothes, whose home was 20 miles (32 kilometres) from Fyvie. Because of this, legend has it, Dame Lilias had died of a broken heart.

Although history and hearsay would appear to part company in their accounts of Seton's behaviour immediately after his wife's death, there can be no doubt that he lost little time in wooing the said Lady Grizel Leslie. Within six months, they were married.

On the night of 27 October, they retired to their temporary bedchamber, a small room at the top of the spiral staircase in the older part of the castle, as their new quarters – in what is now Seton Tower – were not yet finished.

That night, they both heard heavy sighs coming from outside their room; but even though Seton went out to investigate and roused a servant, no intruder was found. With the dawn, however, they discovered a startling indication of the intruder's identity. Carved upside down on the window sill, in neat 3-inch (7-centimetre) high letters, was the name D. LILIES DRUMMOND.

The carving, still clear and quite unworn, is over 50 feet (15 metres) from the ground in the old defensive wall of the castle, which had deliberately been built without any footholds.

Various suggestions have been put forward ever since as to an origin for the carving; but none seems tenable. The precision of the work and the perfection of the lettering show that, however it was done, it took great skill, so that any 'hoax' on the part of Seton or one of his ordinary household can probably be ruled out. Besides, why should the laird do something so calculated to terrify the young wife with whom he was obviously in love? And if he or someone else in the castle did it, why write it upside down?

Seton was the great architect of Fyvie as it stands today, and work is known to have been underway at the time of his second marriage. It has been suggested that one of his masons inscribed the name out of respect for the dead mistress. But, again, why do it upside down on a window-sill and

Another of Lord Fyvie's additions to the castle was the great stone wheel staircase, below. It is on this staircase that the Green Lady, the ghost of the unhappy Dame Lilias, is sometimes seen. She is dressed in a shimmering green gown and her appearance often heralds a death in the family. A portrait, right, that hangs in the castle is said to be of the Green Lady ghost rather than of Dame Lilias: it is dated 1676, 75 years after Dame Lilias died.

where it could be seen only from the interior of the room? Commemorative plaques, consisting of initials and coat of arms, were normally carved on stone and let into the surface of the wall where they could be seen. But the room was not in general use; in fact, it was far from the sumptuous new apartments Seton was then building, and was chosen at the very last moment. To reach the window-sill, it would have been necessary to erect scaffolding – a lengthy process. The mason would then have had to climb the scaffolding and noisily hammer out the deeply incised lettering. Yet, all the newlywed couple heard were 'deep sighs'.

LUMINOUS LADY

Whether natural or supernatural, the mysterious topsy-turvy writing marked the beginning of the haunting of the staircase, and the corridors leading from it, by a luminous 'Green Ladye', as 17th-century documents call her. Naturally, it was presumed that she was Dame Lilias, although a portrait dated 1676 that hangs in the castle, and reputedly that of the ghost, bears only a slight resemblance to the portrait of Seton's first wife. It is clad in a blue-green dress, and a faint iridescence seems to radiate from the enigmatic features.

The 'Green Lady' and her nocturnal rambles up and down the great wheel staircase were periodically documented over the years; and each account tells of the greenish-glow that surrounded her. Sometimes, however, she was seen simply as a flicker of light at the end of a dark corridor. Colonel Cosmo Gordon, fifth Laird of Gordon of Fyvie, who had the castle from 1847 to 1879, recorded that, on one occasion, he was shaken out of bed by unseen hands; while on another night, a wind arose inside the castle – when all outside was quiet – and blew the bedclothes off him and his various guests.

Presumably, Dame Lilias was in a boisterous mood on that occasion.

The Gordons came to Fyvie in 1733, and the apparition was seen so many times that they came to adopt the 'Green Lady' as their own, believing that her existence was personal to them. One story told by Colonel Cosmo Gordon seems to bear this out. A lady and her maid, named Thompson, happened to be staying for a weekend. At breakfast one morning, the visitor remarked that her maid had seen a lady she did not know in a green dress going up the principal staircase.

'It must have been the Green Lady,' said the Colonel, adding rather possessively, 'though she only appears to a Gordon.'

'Oh,' exclaimed the visitor, 'I always call my maids "Thompson" as a matter of course. Her real name *is* Gordon!'

Just before he died, Cosmo Gordon saw a figure beckoning him from the shadows of a room, and took the apparition to be an omen of his own impending death. A few days later, his younger brother saw the 'Green Lady' walking towards him in the gloomy December light that shone through the inscribed window. As she reached him, she curtseyed. The following morning Cosmo died.

ILLUMINATED PICTURES

During the First World War, a Canadian army officer left an account of his brush with supernatural forces at Fyvie, the most impressive in the castle's annals. A mining engineer by profession, he was formerly a complete sceptic: 'If anyone had told me before I came here that there were such things as ghosts or anything supernatural, I should have looked upon that man as an arrant fool,' he said.

On the first night of his stay, the officer retired to bed and fell asleep. Some time later, he woke up to find the light on, or so he thought, and got up to switch it off: 'But so doing, to my amazement, I found that I had switched it on. I extinguished it once more, but the light remained. The room was illuminated from some other cause, and as I watched, the light got gradually brighter. It was like little flames playing around the pictures, and I could see the colours of the pictures quite distinctly.'

The same phenomenon occurred every night until the end of his stay; and although no apparition apart from the strange light appeared, there was, said the Canadian, a feeling of 'someone or something in the room – something I wanted to hit.'

Lord Leith of Fyvie, who bought the castle in 1889 and died in 1925, had not only seen the same phenomenon, but had it investigated scientifically. At the same time, he had the only known 'weeping stone' examined. The latter proved to be a form of porous sandstone, which absorbed and exuded moisture by a natural process; but no 'scientific explanation' for the carving on the window-sill, or the wanderings of the 'Green Lady' and her luminescence, was forthcoming. Since Lord Leith's death, the 'Green Lady' has been glimpsed only periodically by visitors, but the enigmatic carving remains for all to see. Whatever the truth behind the stories of Fyvie Castle, Lord Leith's motto on the subject seems to have been a sound one: 'Never combat the supernatural,' he told a guest. 'Meet it without fear, and it will not trouble you.'

AN ATTRACTIVE HOUSE ON NEW YORK'S LONG ISLAND BECAME FIRST THE SCENE OF A SERIES OF SADISTIC MURDERS AND, SUBSEQUENTLY, A PLAYGROUND FOR MALEVOLENT PARANORMAL FORCES. HOW DID THESE TERRIFYING EVENTS COME ABOUT?

AMITYVILLE – HORROR OR HOAX?

Early in the morning of 13 November 1974, a young New Yorker, 24-year-old Ronald DeFeo, ran screaming hysterically into a bar near his Ocean Avenue home, in Long Island's district of Amityville. Someone, he sobbed, had broken into the DeFeo house and slaughtered the six members of his family. When the police reached the house, they discovered his mother, father, two sisters and two brothers shot dead in their beds. DeFeo's claim that the crime had been committed by an intruder was not taken seriously, and he was arrested and charged with the murders.

At his trial, the prosecution maintained that DeFeo's motive was a wild attempt to lay his hands on life insurance worth $200,000, plus the considerable funds in the family cash box. Defence attorney William Weber countered with a plea of insanity, backed up by testimony from a string of psychiatrists. But the jury rejected that plea, and Ronald DeFeo was sentenced to six consecutive life-terms.

When the trial was over, the DeFeo house was put up for sale. It was an imposing three-storey residence, built in the Dutch Colonial style in 1928, and with its garage, boathouse and swimming pool made a substantial property that should have commanded a high figure. Instead, in view of its unhappy history, the house agents offered it at the bargain price of $80,000. Even so, it remained empty for nearly a year before the Lutz family moved in on 18 December 1975.

Recently married, George Lutz was a 28-year-old ex-marine who ran a land surveying company. His wife Kathy, a divorcee, was kept fully occupied looking after her two small sons and five-year-old daughter. The large rambling house seemed the ideal place for a young family. But only a month later, the Lutzes were to flee from it – victims, they said, of a relentless, nameless terror.

The full story of their ordeal was told in the book *The Amityville Horror* by Jay Anson, which was based on many interviews with the Lutzes themselves. This book became a best-seller and was acclaimed as 'one of the most terrifying true cases ever of haunting and possession by demons'.

any human being. Soon, it began to dawn on the new owners that, far from being the home of their dreams, 112 Ocean Avenue was a nightmare house, haunted by malignant forces.

Kathy Lutz was the first to be truly terrorized by the entities. Invisible arms embraced her and tried to gain possession of her body; she sensed she was going to die. Others, too, were feeling the effects of the 'horror'. A priest who had befriended the Lutzes was struck down by a mysterious, enervating infection, and the rectory where he lived also became filled with a horrible smell that drove all the occupants out into the open air.

At Ocean Avenue, George's experience of the presences was the sound of a marching band, boots thumping and horns blaring. Although he was convinced there must have been at least 50 musicians, not one was ever seen, yet the furniture was found pushed back against the walls, as if to make room for the invading marchers.

In a scene from the film The Amityville Horror, *the Lutzes' house at 112 Ocean Avenue,* far left, *assumes a menacing aspect at night when the two top-floor windows seem to stare out like baleful eyes. Another manifestation of the malignant forces in the house is the loathsome slime that Kathy, played by Margot Kidder in the film, finds covering the mirror in her bedroom,* above left. *Later, George, played by James Brolin, and Kathy are awakened in the middle of the night to find the heavy front door wrenched wide open, apparently from the inside and hanging from its one remaining hinge,* left.

According to the account in the book, trouble at the Ocean Avenue home began with overpoweringly foul stenches that pervaded the house. The bathroom fittings became stained with a black slime, which no household cleaner would remove. Then came the flies – hundreds of them, swarming into a second-floor bedroom.

On one occasion, the massive front door was discovered wrenched open and hanging from its one remaining hinge. George felt constantly chilled to the bone, despite the huge blazing fire that roared in the living room. It also seemed that a four-feet (1.2 metre) high ceramic lion began moving around the house without human help.

Then the Lutzes spotted cloven-hoof tracks in the snow around the house – they led directly to the garage and stopped dead in front of the door. The door itself had been almost torn off its metal frame, a feat requiring strength far beyond that of

Another manifestation of the sadistic forces were the hideously painful, red weals that erupted on Kathy's body, as if she had been slashed with a red-hot poker. There were also, according to the book, levitations, drastic personality changes, and the appearance of demons.

On 14 January 1976, the Lutzes left the house at Amityville, never to return. But according to the account of their experiences related in *The Amityville Horror: Part 2* (a sequel to the first book), the evil presences followed them to their new home, where they apparently stayed 'coiled malevolently round them'.

If all this is true, it is a grim and horrifying story. But it is so like fiction that it prompts the reader to ask whether there was ever an authentic horror in the first place. Independent researchers who have investigated the facts have all emphatically answered 'no'.

As he told Jay Anson, author of the book The Amityville Horror, *George Lutz, above, felt continually cold in the house, despite a high level of heating. He was also plagued by the sound of a brass band that nobody could see. Soon, he began to identify with multiple murderer Ronald DeFeo, above right, whom he imagined he resembled physically. His wife Kathy, right, suffered from painful red weals all over her body, as if she had been burned with a red-hot poker.*

'' PEOPLE IN AMITYVILLE HAVE

LONG SINCE BECOME ACCUSTOMED TO

THE PLACE, BUT THEY ALSO TEND TO

AVOID IT, ESPECIALLY AT NIGHT...

IF YOU LIVE IN AMITYVILLE, YOU JUST

MIND YOUR BUSINESS AND LET THAT

PIECE OF LAND BE. **''**

HANS HOLZER,

THE SECRET OF AMITYVILLE

Dr Stephen Kaplan, director of the Parapsychology Institute of America, said, after months of study and many interviews with those involved in the affair of 'the Amityville Horror':

'We found no evidence to support any claim of a haunted house. What we did find is a couple who had purchased a house that they economically could not afford. It is our professional opinion that the story of the haunting is mostly fiction.'

Jerry Solfvin, of the Psychical Research Foundation, wrote that the case 'wasn't interesting to us because the reports were confined to subjective responses from the Lutzes, and these were not at all... characteristic of those cases.'

POLICE DENIAL

The most damaging report of all originated with investigators Rick Moran and Peter Jordan who visited Amityville and interviewed people mentioned in the book. Among their findings was the fact that the police denied investigating the house while the Lutzes were in residence, although the book describes Sergeant Cammaroto touring it and even inspecting a 'secret room' in the basement.

Father Mancuso (in real life, Father Pecorara), the priest who appears throughout the book, flatly denied that he had ever entered the Lutzes' home; so the tale about him blessing the building (and the phantom voice that ordered him out) must be quite bogus. The pastor of the Sacred Heart rectory also dismissed the Lutzes' yarn about a 'disgusting odour that permeated the rectory' – the alleged 'scent of the devil' – which was supposed to have driven the priests out of their building.

In fact, very little in the book stood up under scrutiny. Local handymen knew nothing of the paranormal damages they were supposed to have repaired. And far from being driven out of the house by hauntings, it appeared that the real reasons for the Lutzes leaving their home were much more prosaic: a cash crisis and a near-breakdown.

The Lutzes responded to these revelations with what came over as bluff and bluster. But it is worth noting that they repeatedly avoided a confrontation with their critics; and in fact their original accounts were only about things felt and sensed, not about objective phenomena.

Indeed, it was Ronald DeFeo's defence attorney, William Weber, who first pushed the couple into the limelight. DeFeo had spoken of a voice that urged him to kill, and Weber hoped to win a new trial for him by establishing that the house contained some force able to influence the behaviour of the inhabitants. Pinning his hopes on the Lutzes, he won them time on New York's *Ten O'Clock News* television programme.

Although at the outset, Weber's involvement seemed to be on a purely professional basis, he admitted that he had helped to sensationalize the Lutzes' story. In a press release on 27 July 1979, he said: 'We created this horror story over many bottles of wine that George was drinking. We were really playing with each other.'

But the case against the Lutzes does not rest solely on these testimonies by outsiders. The Lutzes themselves gave ample evidence of their unreliability in major interviews, as we shall see in a forthcoming feature.

A HOUSE POSSESSED?

THE SENSATIONAL SAGA OF ENTITIES THAT POSSESSED A HOUSE IN AMITYVILLE, NEW YORK, SEEMS TO HAVE UNDERGONE A STRANGE TRANSFORMATION AT EVERY TELLING

Jay Anson, left, wrote a dramatic account of the hauntings at 112 Ocean Avenue, below, from information supplied by George and Kathy Lutz, in his book The Amityville Horror. In a postscript to the book, he said he was convinced the Lutzes were telling the truth.

The sinister story of a house haunted by malignant forces has chilled many people since it was first published in Jay Anson's book *The Amityville Horror* in 1978. In the preface to the book, it is claimed that the story is 'a documentary told by the family and the priest who actually experienced what is reported'; but many independent investigators have since claimed that the events related are almost entirely fictitious.

Fortunately for the truth, George and Kathy Lutz, who lived at the 'horror' house at 112 Ocean Avenue between 18 December 1975 and 14 January 1976, left a trail of revealing evidence behind them that does not agree with the account they later gave to author Jay Anson. In an article published in *Long Island Press* on 17 January 1976, just a few days after the Lutzes had fled from the

house, George sets out his experiences; but his story centres around things that were sensed rather than seen and is completely at odds with later accounts of flying objects, moving couches and wailing noises. The only physical phenomenon he mentions is a window that opened of its own accord; but later investigations showed that the counterweights were merely too heavy! At that date, the Amityville happenings were purely subjective and scarcely worthy of note.

A year later, George produced a new version of events, which journalist Paul Hoffman wrote up for the April 1977 issue of America's *Good Housekeeping* magazine. This text flatly contradicts the earlier account and conflicts with the Anson story as well.

The *Good Housekeeping* account begins with a Roman Catholic priest blessing the house. When he leaves, the priest warns the Lutzes about one of the bedrooms, saying: 'Don't let anyone sleep in there. Keep the door closed. Spend as little time as possible in there.' But this does not tally with the book. There, the priest's alleged advice about not using the room is given one week after the blessing – and following a whole series of nasty events.

The next person to be affected by the house is Kathy Lutz's aunt, described in the *Good Housekeeping* article as a 'normally placid ex-nun'. When she comes to visit, she behaves quite out of character and becomes hostile towards George, who says she 'sat there and cut me down for three hours'. In the book, this incident seems to have been reshaped to make it more dramatic. The aunt can stand being in the house only for a very short while: she simply inspects it, refuses to enter certain rooms, and leaves. In fact, we are told that she 'hadn't been in the house for more than half an hour when she decided it was time to go'.

In a scene from the film The Amityville Horror, *George, below, played by James Brolin, is haunted by a vision of killer Ronald DeFeo, with whom he is becoming obsessed. Just before leaving the house for ever, a storm-drenched Kathy, bottom, played by Margot Kidder, returns for the last time to the children's room on the second floor, the scene of some of the most alarming phenomena.*

A similar re-vamping technique is used on the 'old crone' incident. In *Good Housekeeping*, George says that, on Saturday, 10 January 1976, he woke at night with 'a compulsion to flee the house'. He yelled at his wife and shook her, but could not wake her. Then, as he watched, his sleeping wife 'turned into a 90-year-old woman'. Her hair became 'old and dirty', she dribbled, and creases and crow's feet appeared on her face; 'it took several hours before she returned to her normal self.'

When this story makes its appearance in Jay Anson's book, it undergoes significant changes. First, it is placed some days earlier, on Wednesday, 7 January. George does not wake up wanting to flee the house; on the contrary, he is unable to get to sleep, and in this wide-awake state feels an urge to go out to the local tavern for a beer. When he turns to speak to Kathy, he finds her levitating 'almost a foot [30 centimetres] above him'. He pulls her down on to the bed, where she wakes. And it is

" BECAUSE OF THE UNCERTAINTIES CONNECTED WITH THE PARANORMAL, I... WOULD BE REMISS NOT TO WARN READERS AGAINST... AN ARROGANCE THAT PROFESSES A GRASP OF THE UNKNOWN... THE WISE MAN KNOWS THAT HE DOES NOT KNOW – AND THE PRUDENT MAN RESPECTS WHAT HE DOES NOT CONTROL. **"**

REVD. JOHN J. NICOLA, PREFACE TO THE AMITYVILLE HORROR BY JAY ANSON

whole thing off. But it is known that George Lutz was a man with difficulties. After his first marriage broke up, he tried group therapy, then turned to transcendental meditation. Things seemed to improve for a while after his second marriage, but he was facing a crisis even before he moved to Amityville: Kathy's two sons had tried to run away, his business was in difficulties, and he had problems with the tax people. What is more, rather than cutting back on expenditure, George decided to buy a house that was way beyond his means.

Once the family was settled in the new house, matters fast came to a head. George became apathetic: he didn't wash or shave, and he stopped going to the office. In the book, he describes how he would lie awake at night, worrying.

'A second marriage with three children, a new house with a big mortgage. The taxes in Amityville were three times higher than in Deer Park. Did he really need that new speedboat? How the hell was he going to pay for all of this? The construction business was lousy on Long Island... '

then, while awake, that she turns into a 90-year-old woman. In this version, the state lasts only for a minute or two – not several hours.

As described in the book, this levitation was the second of three. The first took place on 4 January, when Kathy floated 'two feet [60 centimetres] above the bed'. A further levitation took place after the Lutzes left the house, when they were staying with Kathy's mother on 15 January. On this occasion, both George and Kathy floated around at the same time. Yet nothing was ever said about these remarkable levitations in *Good Housekeeping*. The only time levitation is mentioned is when George describes waking on the night of 11 January, to find 'Kathy sliding across the bed, as if by levitation' – a very different matter from 'floating in the air'.

The ultimate horror, however, is the series of visitations by an entity variously described as a 'gigantic [hooded] figure in white' and a 'demon with horns' with half its face shot away. Yet, in *Good Housekeeping*, there is not one hint of his visits. There is a passing mention, however, of Kathy seeing 'some eyes at the window', which she described as 'red, beady eyes'. When this story reaches the book, it becomes a point of high drama.

Set in a second-storey bedroom at night, this dramatic episode, as described by Anson, has the Lutzes' young daughter pointing to a window where George and Kathy see 'two fiery, red eyes. No face, just the mean, little eyes of a pig', looking in. Kathy rushes at the window 'screaming in an unearthly voice'. She smashes the glass with a chair and they hear an 'animal cry of pain, a loud squealing – and the eyes were gone'. The squealing continues for a while outside the house. But George does not go out to look for the flying pig; instead, he comforts his wife, who sobs: 'It's been here all the time. I wanted to kill it. I wanted to kill it!'

The story has obviously undergone a remarkable transformation. And similar 'improvements' are apparent throughout the book. Coupled with the findings of independent investigators, this evidence suggests that the whole bizarre tale is a fabrication.

Without a confession from the Lutzes, it will probably never be quite clear what started the

In another scene from the film George, above, hatchet in hand, challenges the demonic forces plaguing the house. After visiting the house to bless it, Father Delaney, right, played in the film by Rod Steiger, discovers that his palms are raw and bleeding.

All this worry soon took its toll. George began to blame his inertia, his bad temper and his problems on the house. When he was short with his employees, or when he hit the children, it was the fault of the bad vibrations from the house, not his own lack of control. In this frame of mind, he began to identify with the murderer Ronald DeFeo. Indeed, he became convinced he was DeFeo's physical double, recording that, when he first saw DeFeo's picture, it could have been his own.

And if he was the physical double of a psychopath, why not the mental double, too? There is little doubt that George felt black, murderous thoughts in the house in Ocean Avenue, but these arose from his own plight and frustrations.

After leaving Amityville, George became more and more enmeshed in his morbid fantasies, and the situation began to spin out of control. The meeting with Anson offered an opportunity to crystallize his sinister imaginings in profitable form. But to become a best-seller, the story had to pose as fact. As fiction, it is debatable whether the book would even have covered its printing costs.

A POTENT MIXTURE OF MURDER, MAYHEM AND A DASH OF MYSTERY FREQUENTLY ENLIVENS THE HISTORY OF MANY BRITISH PUBS. WHAT LIES BEHIND THESE INTRIGUING TALES OF THE TROUBLESOME SPIRITS THAT ARE SAID TO HAUNT A NUMBER OF BRITISH INNS?

The public house is not only one of the most popular institutions of the British way of life, but also one of the most haunted. In the mid-1970s, when writing the book *The English Pub*, Michael Jackson, together with Frank Smyth, carried out a survey among the 'big six' combines and the two dozen or so independent breweries that between them control most of the country's estimated 70,000 inns. To a question concerning the number of pubs traditionally said to be haunted, the reply was rather surprising: every brewer claimed to have ghosts on his licensed premises. An independent brewer in the north, for instance,

HAUNTED TAVERNS

boasted that he had three haunted pubs (a quarter of the houses he then owned), while the mighty Bass-Charrington group said that their ghosts were 'too numerous to mention'. A West Country brewery said that 'about one in five' of their pubs had, at one time or another, been associated with supernatural phenomena. The prevailing tone of all the replies was one of quiet pride: ghosts, after all, are part of the national heritage and are usually good for business.

The public house is a unique institution found only in England, Wales and some parts of Scotland. It is totally unlike the traditional bars and bothies of Scotland and Ireland, or the drinking places of America and Europe. Older pubs are quite as hallowed by time as the churches with which they often stand cheek-by-jowl (and have certainly overtaken them in popularity). It is therefore perhaps not so surprising that many of them have acquired a

The infamous Lord Chief Justice Jeffreys, right, was captured on Old Wapping Stairs, above, behind the Town of Ramsgate pub when he was trying to escape to France in 1688. He died in prison before being brought to trial, but it is the stairs that his ghost haunts. It has been seen there by many people, including the Thames river police.

Near the Marsden Grotto tavern, right, a gruesome incident occurred in the 18th century, and mysterious wails are still heard to this day.

reputation for being haunted. Nevertheless, it is unwise, for obvious reasons, to accept every pub ghost story as a truthful account.

A case in point is that of Madge Gill, the 'primitive' painter from London's East End, who died in the 1960s. One day, during the 1930s, she was sitting in a pub in Whitechapel (according to her own testimony) when she became aware of the presence of a ghost. This spirit said its name was 'Mirinarest', and urged her to draw some pictures under its guidance. She subsequently produced hundreds of finely detailed drawings, full of weird patterns and tormented faces. An exhibition of her 'spirit drawings' was even held in a London gallery after her death.

'But,' asserted one of her former drinking companions, 'gin was the only spirit that moved her.'

Certainly, the combined effects of alcohol and primitive lighting must frequently have contributed to ghostly pub lore in days gone by; with a dash of authentic history, the supernatural cocktail is complete. The tale of the Marsden Grotto pub, on the north-east coast of England, provides an example.

GHOSTLY GROANS

The story goes that, in 1782, a retired miner, appropriately named Jack the Blaster, widened the natural caverns in the 100-foot (30-metre) high limestone cliffs opposite Marsden Rock in order to use them as a base for smuggling operations. When threatened with betrayal by a colleague, who had the equally appropriate name of John the Jibber, Jack rigged a tub on a pulley to the high roof of the caverns and kept John a prisoner in it, lowering him only occasionally for food. The motive behind this arrangement seems to have been to save murdering the would-be traitor. But he died in the tub, anyway. In 1850, an enterprising gamekeeper saw the possibilities of the old smuggler's cave as a beer cellar and built the present inn on to it. But the pleasures of drinking were to be spoiled by ghostly wails and groans coming from the caves, usually late at night. These can still be heard, it is said, and are attributed to the death torments of 'awd John, jibberin away'. But fast tides crashing against a honeycombed cliff face and brown ale may also play a part in the phenomenon.

In rural communities, where the inn has been a focal point of life for generations, it tends to become a repository of local lore and legend. Tales are told and re-told, polished and embellished. The story of an inn on Dartmoor, in Devon, clearly illustrates this.

In the late 1960s, the novelist Gordon Williams rented a cottage on the edge of Dartmoor to research a novel. His 'local' was the Warren House Inn, high on the moor between Widecombe-in-the-Moor and Moretonhampstead.

The inn, he was told, had once been haunted, but the ghosts had disappeared along with the practice of 'corpse transportation'. Before Widecombe had a consecrated burial ground, bodies had been carried across the moor to the churchyard at Moretonhampstead for burial. Treacherous weather and deep snowfalls are a feature of moorland winters; and when the pall-bearers were defeated by such conditions, they would leave the bodies, pickled in brine, in great cider vats in the inn's cellars to await the coming of spring. One local inhabitant told Williams that all this had happened 'in my grandfather's time' and that the innkeeper was 'fair troubled by the spirits' until a churchyard was opened in Widecombe.

Williams was intrigued by this story and checked it out in the British Library. He found that the tale was indeed based on fact; but the last 'corpse transportation', it seemed, had taken place centuries ago.

Apart from the influence of drink and legend, there remain several potent reasons why a pub should become the scene of a haunting. A phantom seeking the lost comforts of life on Earth could do worse than frequent an inn. And if ghosts are merely psychic 'replays' of cataclysmic events, the pub is certainly exposed over the years to a far more varied spectrum of human emotions than, say, the village shop. In many instances, a pub haunting is a product of murder and mayhem. Two of London's most famous haunted pubs, the Grenadier and the Town of Ramsgate, are cases in point.

AN INVISIBLE HAND

The Grenadier, in Belgravia's Old Barrack Yard, began life in the 18th century as an officers' mess for the Coldstream and Grenadier Guards. In the early 19th century, a young subaltern, caught cheating at cards, was reputedly beaten so severely with horsewhips by his fellow officers that he died. Although documentary evidence for the incident is fragmentary, there is good reason to believe that it did take place around 1820, and that the Duke of Wellington himself was involved in the subsequent cover-up.

There is no record of the month in which the manslaughter is supposed to have taken place but, according to reports going back at least to the 1880s, it is always in September that strange happenings occur at the pub. These have included an icy coldness in the cellar, the sensation of an invisible body bumping violently into bystanders, and a variety of noises. On one occasion in the early 1970s, a barman was struck by an antique military helmet that hurtled from its place on the wall; and some years earlier, the cellarman had been grabbed by a powerful unseen hand and pulled backwards down the cellar steps. Although admitting to its presence, the Grenadier management are reluctant to advertise their ghost, perhaps fearing that it will deter people from working there.

The Warren House Inn, left, on Dartmoor, was reputedly once haunted by spirits of the dead bodies that were left there, pickled in brine, when the weather was too bad to carry them over the moor for burial in Moretonhampstead churchyard, right.

At the Town of Ramsgate pub, in Wapping High Street, beside the river Thames, the ghost is said to be that of Lord Chief Justice George Jeffreys, the infamous 'hanging judge' who presided at the Bloody Assizes of 1685. At these trials, hundreds of people implicated in the Monmouth rebellion – an insurrection by the Duke of Monmouth against King James II – were executed or transported to slavery. The modern frontage of the pub dates from the 1930s; but the main fabric, the landing stage and Wapping Old Stairs (leading down from the pub to the river) are at least 300 years old.

At the Grenadier pub in Belgravia, below, a young Guards officer was supposedly whipped to death for cheating at cards. The ghostly legacy from this manslaughter includes bumps, noises and a sensation of icy coldness.

When James II fled the country in 1688, Jeffreys also tried to escape, disguised as a sailor. But he was recognized and arrested on Wapping Old Stairs and taken to the Tower of London, where he died the following year before being brought to trial. Possibly the panic he felt was so strong that it became 'imprinted' on the place; but his spirit seems to have changed in appearance over the years. While many witnesses have identified the judge's grim features from contemporary portraits, others have reported seeing a cavalier in a periwig and velvet breeches, or a grey-haired old man in a long white nightshirt. Nevertheless, sightings have been reported over so many years and by so many witnesses (including the Thames river police) that this tavern phantom deserves to be rated as genuine.

CURSED CHAIR

If some people who have encountered the Grenadier ghost have been bruised or buffeted, many of the victims of a pub ghost in North Yorkshire have been even more unfortunate. The Busby Stoop Inn at Kirby Wiske, a village near Thirsk, takes its odd name from an 18th-century owner and his 'stoop', or tall chair. It is the chair that is haunted, or rather cursed. The disreputable Busby appears to have eked out his living by coin-clipping, thieving and receiving stolen goods; and he was eventually sentenced to death for the murder of a female relative. As he was dragged from his inn, he swore that anyone who sat in his 'stoop' would perish as violently and suddenly as he was about to die.

Simon Theakston, whose brewery owned the pub until 1978, expressed the belief that: 'The legend may be odd and vague, but it is a matter of record that, in the last 200 years or so, death has struck anyone who dared to sit in the chair within a very short time.' He said that many who sat in the chair were dead within days, or even hours. Eventually, the chair was moved out of harm's way.

It has to be said that many of the chair victims of the last few decades could be categorized as 'high risk' anyway. They included an RAF fighter pilot (who was killed the following day), a motorist (who crashed the next day and died of his injuries), a motorcyclist (killed shortly after leaving the pub), a holiday hitch-hiker (knocked down and killed two days later) and a local man in his late thirties (who died of a heart attack the following night). But the odds against all of these people dying so soon after sitting in the Busby stoop must be high enough to suggest that their passing was no mere coincidence.

The ferocious bull terrier whose stuffed head, above left, guards the bar in the Star Inn, above, at Ingatestone, Essex, died in 1914. Its ghost is said to haunt the passage leading to the bar.

Stories of the supernatural and 'real-life' psychical research also emphasize the adverse reactions of some animals to certain types of ghostly phenomena. The Star Inn at Ingatestone in Essex, for example, is said to be haunted by a dog that seems to appear only to other dogs. In life, it was a bull terrier, which lived in the inn from about 1900 to 1914. A notorious fighter, it killed several neighbourhood dogs, and was never defeated. When it died of old age, its stuffed head was hung in the bar parlour; and since that day, its ferocious spirit has guarded the passageway giving access to the bar from the side of the pub. A former landlord said of his experience with this canine spectre: 'The moment my dog set foot in the passage, she growled, stiffened, and up went her bristles like a hedgehog. She was not only threatening something – but she was being threatened herself. She was dead scared.'

The phantom bull terrier not only continues to 'see off' its earthly kin, but also seems to deter local burglars: although pubs are known to be a prime target in rural Essex, the Star Inn has never had a break-in.

But perhaps the most ironic of pub hauntings is that of The Bull at Long Melford in Suffolk, a few miles from Borley Rectory and its alleged ghosts. The Bull, a 17th-century coaching inn, was used as a base by ghost-hunter Harry Price during his connection with the Borley Rectory 'phenomena'. In 1977, the Enfield Psychical Research Group also adopted the inn as their base, and watering-hole, when they began making tape recordings in Borley Church. 'One evening,' said a member, 'we had assembled in the bar and I'd just commented that it can't have changed much since Price's time, when a cocktail shaker whizzed off the shelf and clattered to the floor. The barmaid sighed, picked it up and said to me: "Now look what you've done!" Apparently, psychokinetic happenings occur there fairly regularly. Perhaps Harry resents his exposure as a fraud and is making a point!'

The cursed stoop chair at the Busby Stoop Inn, North Yorkshire, left, is not as welcoming as it looks. So many people who sat in the stoop died soon afterwards that eventually the brewery moved the chair out of harm's way.

HAUNTING OF A SCOTTISH CASTLE

SHRIEKS, GROANS, HEAVY FOOTSTEPS AND THE UNCANNY SOUND OF SOMETHING BEING DRAGGED ALONG THE FLOOR MADE NIGHTS AT A LONELY CASTLE A TERRIFYING EXPERIENCE FOR THE OCCUPANTS. NO RATIONAL EXPLANATION HAS BEEN FOUND TO THIS DAY

The 17th-century painting of King Charles II, left, is now in the National Portrait Gallery, London. Because a massive carved bed had reputedly been slept in by Charles II, the room at Penkaet Castle containing it became known as the King Charles room. Many of the paranormal happenings at the castle, right, were connected with this room.

The four-poster bed in the main bedroom of Penkaet Castle, left, had been a present from students to Professor Holbourn, who bought the castle in 1923. The masks on either side of the bottom of the bed were said to be replicas of the death mask of Charles I, and the bed was believed to have been used by his son, Charles II. On several occasions, the bedclothes were found rumpled as if the bed had been slept in, even though no one had been in the room.

On a windy weekend in March 1946, a party of students gathered at Penkaet Castle in Scotland to rehearse a play they intended to perform at Edinburgh College of Art. After the first day of rehearsal, supper was served and the party retired to bed. Two of the girls, Susan Hart and Carol Johnstone, were put in the King Charles room, so called because it contained a massive carved four-poster bed, reputedly slept in by Charles II.

On either side of the bed a candle burned, throwing long shadows across the cavernous room. Although there was an oil heater, it was extremely cold, so cold that the girls found it impossible to get to sleep.

About midnight, both girls heard a sound, which they said was like 'something trundling across the floor above' or 'something going down a slope'. The strange sound was repeated from time to time, and they also heard footsteps.

At about 2 a.m., a new phenomenon presented itself. On the wall opposite the bed, they noticed a large, dark brown stain. It was on the right-hand side of the fireplace, giving the impression that part of the paper had come away from the wall and was now hanging down. The following night, to their

surprise, the patch had disappeared. Although the girls experimented with the candles in an attempt to produce a shadow of the same shape and position, they were unsuccessful.

This was not the first time that Penkaet Castle had been the scene of inexplicable manifestations. Dating from the beginning of the 16th century, it stands near Haddington, Lothian. It is virtually unmodernised and retains many of its original historic furnishings. And there is a legend that a former owner, John Cockburn, killed his relative John Seton, and his troubled conscience is said to cause his ghost to haunt the place.

In the early 1920s, the castle was bought by Professor and Mrs Holbourn, who soon began to experience strange phenomena. 'When we first came here in 1923,' Mrs Holbourn was reported as saying in the *Journal of the American Society for Psychical Research*, 'we were often disturbed by the sounds of heavy footsteps going about the house, and the sound of something heavy and soft being dragged along. Various people who occupied the house [in our absence] complained of hearing shrieks and groans, and that doors which were shut and even locked at night were found open in the morning. One girl was so terrified that she refused to sleep alone.'

Sometimes, when Professor and Mrs Holbourn found the noises too persistent and annoying, the professor would admonish 'John', telling him he was behaving childishly and asking him to stop. The sounds would cease at once.

MUSIC AND MOVEMENT

While carols were being sung in the music room at Christmas 1923, a piece of wood carved with the family crest was seen to lean forward from the wall, 'hesitate' and then return to its former position. Two years later, a friend occupied the room containing the King Charles bed, and heard someone moving about on the ground floor during the night. She and the professor searched downstairs but could find no one. On their return to the first floor, they heard, from the room above, the sound of someone turning over in the bed that the friend had left.

Ten years later, when a Mrs Carstairs, recuperating from an illness, was sleeping in the King Charles bed, Mrs Holbourn's brother, who was in the room below, was wakened by urgent knocks apparently coming from overhead. Thinking that Mrs Carstairs had fallen out of bed and was knocking for help, he woke Mrs Holbourn, who found the lady sleeping soundly in her bed.

Other people (including Professor and Mrs Holbourn) spending the night in the bedroom below the King Charles room also heard sounds of movement from the room above when it was supposed to be empty. Sometimes, it sounded as if furniture was being moved around; and at other times, it sounded as if someone was 'stumbling and groping about the room'.

In 1924, a cousin was staying in the house while the Holbourns were away. One day, he took a visitor to see the King Charles bed and, when they entered the room, they found the bedclothes ruffled – as if the bed had not been made. The cousin mentioned this to the gardener's daughter, Mrs Anderson (whose job it was to make the beds), and

In March 1946, when a party of students spent the night at Penkaet, young Mr Holbourn and his wife slept in the dining room, left, and Mrs Holbourn Senior occupied the music room, bottom. All three were kept awake far into the night by loud, unexplained noises. Later in the year, in July, members of an East Lothian society visited the house. While they were in the library, below, a glass dome covering a model of Penkaet, below left, suddenly disintegrated.

she expressed surprise, maintaining that she had in fact made the King Charles bed that very morning. The incident was dismissed – until it happened again. The cousin took another visitor up to the room, this time someone who wanted to photograph the bed. Again the bedclothes were found to be disarranged, and again Mrs Anderson had to remake the bed. The visitor took his photograph and left, but returned a day or so later to say that the photograph had been under-exposed. When he and the Holbourns' cousin went up to the bedroom so that he could rephotograph the bed, they found that, once again, the bedclothes had been pulled about. This time, after Mrs Anderson had put the bedclothes straight, the cousin took the precaution of locking the two doors leading into the room and checking that the windows were secure. He also placed two bricks against the main door. The following day, the bricks had been moved and the bedclothes were again disarranged. At the time that these strange occurrences took place, the cousin was the only person living in the house.

Another incident that occurred in the very same room concerned a massive antique cabinet, which was very difficult to move. This was found 6 inches (15 centimetres) away from the wall. In addition, a brass jug and basin had been placed on top of the cabinet, and the jug was lying on its side.

In the summer of 1935, Professor Holbourn's son was working late one evening in the workshop on the ground floor. Although it was about 11 p.m., it was only just getting dark, and the son took the job he was working on outside in order to look at it in the fading light. While he was outside, the housekeeper, Betta Leadbetter, came to the window to tell him that someone was taking a bath. She had heard the taps running, someone splashing about in the bath, and later the water running out. As his wife had been in bed since 9 p.m., he decided to investigate.

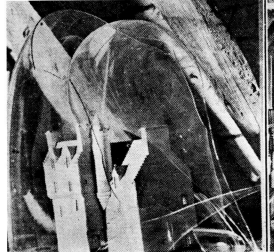

ON THE NIGHT OF HER HUSBAND'S FUNERAL, MRS HOLBOURN SENIOR SAID THAT SHE HAD HEARD FOOTSTEPS COMING DOWN THE PATH OUTSIDE THE HOUSE: SHE ALSO HEARD THE FRONT DOOR OPEN AND SHUT. WHEN HER ELDEST SON INVESTIGATED, HE COULD FIND NOTHING TO ACCOUNT FOR THE SOUNDS.

Legend has it that a former owner of Penkaet Castle, above, a certain John Cockcroft, killed a relative, and that his troubled spirit is responsible for the strange noises and other unaccountable happenings that have so often been reported there. At Christmas 1923, for instance, a piece of wood in the music room, carved with the family crest, was seen by several witnesses to lean forward from the wall, hesitate perceptibly, and then return to its proper place.

When he entered the bathroom, it was full of steam and the mirror and windows completely misted over, although the bath itself was quite dry. No one in the house admitted to having used the bath. The most bizarre feature of this incident concerned the soap. At the time, it was customary for large houses to order soap by the half-hundredweight (25 kilograms). The Penkaet Castle soap was all of one colour. What was found in the bathroom, however, was a square piece of white soap, totally unlike the other soap in the house.

It is well known that domestic animals are acutely sensitive to paranormal phenomena, and another incident at Penkaet Castle bears this out. On the night of her husband's funeral, Mrs Holbourn Senior said that she had heard footsteps coming down the path outside the house: she also heard the front door open and shut. When her eldest son investigated, he could find nothing to account for the sounds. But when he returned, the cat preceded him, showing every sign of being terrified. It took refuge under the table, lashing its tail from side to side.

On another occasion, Professor Holbourn's son heard a scratching sound at one of the two doors leading into the Middle Room. As the household possessed a Siamese cat at the time, he went to open the door for it. To his astonishment, when he was about 3 feet (1 metre) from the door, it suddenly swung wide open, the door at the opposite end of the room did likewise, and a curtain blew outwards, although there was no wind. As he stood there, footsteps were heard down the passage.

Among the students who had come to Penkaet Castle to rehearse their play that weekend in March 1946 was Professor Holbourn's son. Most members of the party arrived on the Saturday and, after a rehearsal and supper, they all retired to bed.

Because the house was so crowded, Mrs Holbourn Senior occupied the music room. During the night she heard, from somewhere above her, loud noises that continued until nearly 3 a.m. Her son and his wife spent the night in the dining room, and they too heard disturbing noises, so severe that they hardly slept at all. It sounded as if the other members of the group were rehearsing the play again – behaviour that seemed quite extraordinary at that time of night.

In the morning, the two girls who had occupied the room above were asked how they had slept. They had been much disturbed by peculiar noises, they complained, but had tried to ignore it all, thinking that perhaps someone was playing a trick.

When Carol and Susan, who had occupied the King Charles room, came down, they told the others about the noises they had heard, and the ghastly stain on the wall. They wondered if a certain William Brown (in the room above theirs) had been playing a trick on them; but when he came down, he said he had slept soundly.

Another member of the party, Margaret Stewart, had slept in the Long Room on the same floor as the King Charles room, sharing it with Carolyn Smith. She had also heard the trundling noise. She said that the room was very cold, and that she had the feeling that they were never quite alone.

STOPPED CLOCKS

Susan Hart had encountered another puzzling phenomenon. She had brought with her a clock, which had been in her possession ever since her schooldays and had never been known to go wrong. At Penkaet, she wound it up, but found that it would not go for more than five minutes continuously throughout her stay at the castle, even though she tried to get it working several times. Mr Holbourn said that he had discovered that any clock placed on the wall between the dining room and the next room would not go. He had also tried hanging a watch on that wall, and it stopped.

Two of the girls, Carol Johnstone and Margaret Stewart, said that they had felt ill throughout their visit. All in all, it seemed that the weekend produced a number of strange and inexplicable events.

On 6 October 1946, a trustee of the Edinburgh Psychic College took a statement from Mrs Holbourn. He also interviewed most of the members of the rehearsal party in Edinburgh on 4 December of that year. William Brown sent a statement from his army camp on 28 January 1947, in which he said that, on the Saturday night in question, all he did after the party retired to bed was to go to the library to look for something to read, go to his room, undress, and lie in bed reading. He said he was asleep long before midnight.

On 29 July 1946, public attention was drawn to the 'entity' that had disturbed the party of young people. It was the day that about 100 members of the East Lothian Antiquarian and Field Naturalists Society had an outing to the castle. In an upper gallery, used as a library, was a glass dome that covered and protected a model of the house. It was about 2 feet (60 centimetres) high, and stood on an oval base about 20 inches (50 centimetres) long. Suddenly, for no apparent reason, and with no one anywhere near it, the dome shattered. Could this perhaps have been a hint from 'John Cockburn' that he was tired of so many visitors?

THE DISCOVERY OF TWO CARVED STONE HEADS IN THE BACK GARDEN OF A HOUSE IN HEXHAM, NORTHUMBERLAND, SEEMED UNREMARKABLE ENOUGH AT FIRST. BUT WHEN THE HEADS TRIGGERED THE APPEARANCE OF A WOLF-MAN, THE NIGHTMARE BEGAN

CURSE OF THE HEXHAM HEADS

One afternoon in February 1972, 11-year-old Colin Robson was weeding the garden of his family's council house in Rede Avenue, Hexham, a market town some 20 miles (32 kilometres) west along the Tyne valley from Newcastle-upon-Tyne. To his surprise, he suddenly uncovered what appeared to be a lump of stone about the size of a tennis ball, with a strange conical protrusion on one side. Clearing the earth from the object, he found that it was roughly carved with human features, and that the conical protrusion was actually meant to be a neck.

Excited by the find, he called to his younger brother Leslie, who was watching from an upstairs

It was in the back garden of a council house in the small town of Hexham in northern England, below left, that two small boys unearthed a pair of crudely carved stone heads, apparently carrying some ancient curse. A distinguished archaeologist suggested that they were around 1,800 years old, and designed to play a part in Celtic head rituals – but Desmond Craigie, left, claimed that he had made them himself.

window. The boys continued to dig, and soon Leslie uncovered a second head.

The stones, which soon became known as the Hexham heads, appeared to be of two distinct types. The first had a skull-like face, seemed to be masculine to everyone who saw it, and was dubbed the 'boy'. It was of a greenish-grey colour, and glistened with crystals of quartz. It was very heavy – heavier than cement or concrete – with hair that appeared to be in stripes running from the front to the back of the head. The other head – the 'girl' – resembled a witch, with wildly bulging eyes and hair that was combed backwards off the forehead in what was almost a bun. There were also traces of a yellow or red pigment in her hair.

After the heads had been unearthed, the boys took them inside the house. It was then that the strange happenings began. The heads would turn round spontaneously, and objects were broken for no apparent reason. It was when the mattress on the bed of one of the Robson daughters was showered with glass that both girls moved out of their room. Meanwhile, at the spot at which the heads had been found, a strange flower bloomed at Christmas and an eerie light glowed.

It could be argued that the events in the Robson household had nothing to do with the appearance of the heads – that they were, instead, poltergeist phenomena triggered by the adolescent children of the Robson family. But the Robsons' next door neighbour, Mrs Ellen Dodd, underwent a truly unnerving experience that could clearly not be explained away so easily. As she recounted:

'I had gone into the children's bedroom to sleep with one of them, who was ill. My ten-year-old son, Brian, kept telling me he felt something touching him. I told him not to be so silly. Then I saw this shape. It came towards me and I definitely felt it touch me on the legs. Then, on all fours, it moved out of the room.'

Ellen Dodd later described the creature that had touched her as 'half human, half sheep-like'. Mrs Robson also recalled that she had heard a sound

The Hexham heads, top, are presumed to be those of a male, left, and a female. A comparison with heads that are known to be modern, above, reveals striking similarities. The head on the left was made by Desmond Craigie, in an attempt to prove that he made the original heads; the one on the right, curiously enough, was made by one of the boys who unearthed the Hexham heads shortly before their discovery.

The figure of the wolf-man, left, which appears in legends throughout the world, is similar in appearance to a creature said to appear in the presence of the Hexham heads.

like a crash as well as screams from next-door on the night in question. Her neighbour told her that the creature that made them was like a werewolf. And when Mrs Dodd went downstairs, she found, that her front door was open. Whatever caused the phenomenon, Ellen Dodd was terrified, and as a result was rehoused by the local council. Eventually, the heads were removed from the Robsons' house, the abode itself was exorcised, and all became quiet in Rede Avenue.

CELTIC RITUALS

Meanwhile, however, a distinguished Celtic scholar, Dr Anne Ross, had become interested in the stones. In an article for *Folklore, Myths and Legends of Britain*, Dr Ross had claimed that the heads were around 1,800 years old and had been designed to play a part in Celtic head rituals. When the heads were banished from the Robsons' house, Dr Ross took charge of them. She recalls what happened next:

'I didn't connect it with the heads then. We always keep the hall light on and the doors kept open because our small son is a bit frightened of the dark, so there's always a certain amount of light coming into our room, and I woke up and felt extremely frightened. In fact, panic-stricken and terribly, terribly cold. There was a sort of dreadful atmosphere of icy coldness all around me. Something made me look towards the door, and as I looked, I saw this thing going out of it.

'It was about six feet [2 metres] high, slightly stooping, and it was black against the white door. It was half-animal and half-man. The upper part, I

" I DIDN'T CONNECT IT WITH THE HEADS THEN ...THE UPPER PART, I WOULD HAVE SAID, WAS WOLF AND THE LOWER PART WAS HUMAN. IT WAS COVERED WITH A KIND OF BLACK, VERY DARK FUR ... I FELT COMPELLED TO RUN AFTER IT. "

would have said, was wolf and the lower part was human. It was covered with a kind of black, very dark fur. It went out and I just saw it clearly and then it disappeared and something made me run after it – a thing I wouldn't normally have done, but I felt compelled to run after it. I got out of bed and I ran, and I could hear it going down the stairs. Then it disappeared toward the back of the house. When I got to the bottom of the stairs, I was terrified.'

That, however, was not the end of the story. A few days later, Dr Ross and her husband arrived home from London one evening to find their teenage daughter in a state of shock. Dr Ross described her daughter's experience as follows:

'She had opened the front door and a black thing, which she described as near a werewolf as anything, jumped over the bannister and landed with a kind of plop. It padded with heavy animal feet, and it rushed toward the back of the house and she felt compelled to follow it. It disappeared in the music room, right at the end of the corridor, and when she got there it had gone. Suddenly, she was terrified. The day the heads were removed from the house everybody, including my husband, said it was as if a cloud had lifted; and since then there hasn't been, really, a trace of it [the paranormal activity].'

Before the heads were removed, however, there were a number of other manifestations of the unwelcome 'lodger'. During those frightening

The complex but ordered shape of copper sulphate crystals, below, reflects the regularity of its subatomic structure. Dr Don Robins, below right, an inorganic chemist and one of the many people to experience the disquieting effect of the Hexham heads, put forward the theory that crystal structures can store information in the form of electrical energy. The Hexham heads contain a high proportion of quartz – a crystalline substance; and Robins explains their apparent ability to induce paranormal effects by suggesting that these are derived from the place in which the heads were made.

months, Dr Ross insisted, the creature appeared to be very real. It was not something shadowy, or only glimpsed out of the corner of the eye. It was noisy, and everyone who came to the house commented on a definite presence of evil. While he never observed it directly, Dr Ross' archaeologist husband was fully aware of his unwelcome 'guest's' presence, although he is not usually sensitive to psychic phenomena. The phenomena ceased after the heads had been removed and the house was exorcised – but not before Dr Ross had disposed of her entire collection of Celtic heads.

HOME-MADE TOYS?

The story took on a new twist in 1972 when Desmond Craigie – then a truck driver – announced that the 'Celtic' heads were actually a mere 16 years old. They had not been fashioned as votive offerings by a head-hunting Celt – for, Craigie claimed, he himself had made them as toys for his daughter, Nancy. He explained that he had lived in the house in Rede Avenue that was now the Robsons' home for around 30 years; indeed, his father had remained a tenant there until the previous year. One day, his daughter had asked him what he did for a living. At that time, Craigie worked with artificial cast stone, making objects such as concrete pillars. In order to explain to his daughter what he did at work, he made three heads especially for her in his lunch break, and took them home for her to play with.

'Nancy played with them as dolls,' he said. 'She would use the silver paper from chocolate biscuits as eyes. One got broken and I threw it in the bin. The others just got kicked around and must have landed up where the lads found them.'

Embarrassed by the publicity that his own handiwork had attracted, Desmond Craigie said he was concerned merely to set the record straight. Speaking of the heads, he said: 'To say that they were old would be conning people'. But Dr Ross was not entirely convinced. 'Mr Craigie's claim is an interesting story... Unless Mr Craigie was familiar with genuine Celtic stone heads, it would be

❝ THE DAY THE HEADS WERE REMOVED FROM THE HOUSE, EVERYBODY – INCLUDING MY HUSBAND – SAID IT WAS AS IF A CLOUD HAD LIFTED; AND SINCE THEN THERE HASN'T BEEN A TRACE OF THE PARANORMAL ACTIVITY. ❞

*In*Focus

HEADS OF THE HOUSEHOLD

Hundreds of stone heads have been found in the north of England, Scotland and mainland Europe. Most of these primitively carved objects can be positively identified as dating from the pre-Roman Celtic period – but some of them are of more mysterious origin.

The Celts of the kingdom of Brigantia, in north-east England, were among those who revered the human head both as a charm against evil and as a fertility symbol, and would set the severed heads of vanquished enemies over the doors of houses and barns. Historians believe that it is an echo of this gruesome cult that lies at the heart of later Celtish veneration of stone heads, such as those shown *left*.

West Yorkshire is particularly rich in such heads. Many are mounted in the walls of buildings, by doorways, on gables, or close to wells, where they seem to be serving their original purpose of warding off evil. But the curious thing is that many of these stone relics of the Celts' grisly cult are no more than a century old. Consciously or unconsciously, Yorkshire men and women have been perpetuating a tradition that is probably more than 2,000 years old.

---

extraordinary for him to make them like this. They are not crude by any means.' Scientific analysis has, surprisingly, been unable to determine the age of the heads.

STORED ENERGIES

If the heads are indeed Celtic, it is easy to imagine that they may be the carriers of some ancient curse. But if they are not, why is it that they appear to provoke paranormal phenomena? The evidence that they do so is strengthened by the testimony of inorganic chemist Don Robins, who has explored the idea that mineral artifacts can store visual images of the people who made them. He also suggested that places and objects can store information that causes specific phenomena to occur – an idea similar to Tom Lethbridge's notion that events can be 'tape-recorded' into the surrounding in which they take place. He has stated, too, that certain minerals have a natural capacity to store information in the form of electrical energy encoded in the lattice structure of their crystals. Summing up this theory, Dr Robins stated:

'The structure of a mineral can be seen as a fluctuating energy network with infinite possibilities of storage and transformation of electronic information. These new dimensions in physical structure may well point the way, eventually, to an understanding of kinetic imagery encoded in stone.'

Robins was interested, too, in reports of sounds that had allegedly accompanied the phenomena and been induced by the presence of the heads, and drew a tentative parallel with a creature from Norse mythology, called the *wulver*, powerful and dangerous, but well-disposed towards mankind unless pro-voked. There are several reports of sightings of this creature in the Shetlands this century.

Dr Robins' interest in the heads prompted him to agree to take charge of them. As he put them in his car in order to take them home, however, and turned on the ignition, all the dashboard electrics suddenly went dead. He turned to look at the heads, telling them firmly to 'Stop it!' – and the car started! No one could have been more surprised than he was.

Back home, Dr Robins, in his turn, began to find the presence of the heads disquieting. Curiously, they seemed, in some way, constantly to be watching him. 'There was no doubt that any influence that the heads possessed came from the girl [head]. I felt most uncomfortable sitting there with them looking at me, and eventually we turned them round. As we did so, I had the distinct impression that the girl's eyes slid round watching me.'

Perhaps disappointingly, however, Dr Robins did not witness any paranormal events that might have been caused by the heads. There were, however, some perturbing moments. One day, leaving the house, he muttered to the heads: 'Let's see something when I get back!' Moments later, he re-entered the house to collect a book he had forgotten. Outside, it was fresh and blustery – but in his study the atmosphere seemed 'almost electric with a stifling, breathless quality'. Attributing the effect to the 'girl' head, he left hurriedly. He found nothing amiss on his return home.

The present whereabouts of the Hexham heads is not known. There also remains the mystery of their age and why they should have produced such startling phenomena.

THE HAUNTING OF BORLEY CHURCH

WERE HARRY PRICE, HIS DETRACTORS AND HIS DEFENDERS CHASING GHOSTS IN THE WRONG PLACE BY CONCENTRATING ON BORLEY RECTORY? THERE IS, IT SEEMS, A CASE FOR A GENUINE HAUNTING ACROSS THE ROAD AT BORLEY CHURCH, STILL UNDER INVESTIGATION

The major part of Borley church, below, was constructed in the 15th century. Should the many who investigated the Borley rectory hauntings have looked here instead?

In all his Borley investigations and writings, Harry Price paid scant attention to the 12th-century church itself. He was aware of a story, told to him by Ethel Bull in 1929, that coffins in the Waldegrave family vault under the church had been mysteriously moved at some time during the 19th century, but he made little attempt to follow up the matter. Thus, Price may have missed his real chance to confront the paranormal: for, since the early

1970s, unexplained events in and around the church – many of them recorded on tape – have proved to be far more baffling than anything that happened in the old rectory.

The manor of 'Barlea' – the Anglo-Saxon for 'boar's pasture' – was mentioned in the Domesday Book, at which time a wooden church served the locality; and the south wall of the present church contains remnants of the flint and rubble building erected in the 12th century. The chancel, the north wall of the nave, and the west tower were added in the 15th century, followed a hundred years later by the red brick south porch.

In the little churchyard itself, planted around with clipped yews and horse chestnut trees, lie the graves of the Bull family. Vandals have broken the stone cross on that of the Rev. Harry Bull, the Victorian rector who drowsed away his last days in the summer-house and who reported seeing a ghostly nun and phantom coach. Geoffrey Croom-Hollingsworth, leader of a small psychical research group at Harlow, Essex, believed, as a result of his investigations, that the cause of the rector's death in 1927 was syphilis. Advanced syphilis is accompanied by a constant drowsiness, during which the sufferer hallucinates – a fact that would explain the rector's 'visions' neatly. But for Croom-Hollingsworth, this was not the whole answer, for he and an assistant, Roy Potter, claimed to have observed the phantom nun themselves.

Croom-Hollingsworth came upon the Borley controversy in the 1960s and decided to examine the facts. He and his group therefore began a series of vigils at Borley. Like subsequent investigators, they chose to keep watch at night to avoid interruption. Over a period of years, in very differing weather

The Enfield Parapsychical Research Group are seen at Borley church, above left. Ronald R. Russell, far right, a founding member, tended towards Price's side in the controversy over Borley's hauntings. But the group found the church itself of most interest and carried out many tests with cameras and sound equipment, as in the photograph, right.

The Reverend Harry Bull's grave in Borley churchyard was subject to vandalism, as shown above right.

conditions and at different times of year, they heard an assortment of noises – raps, heavy panting and furniture being moved. On one occasion, while in the orchard, something huge and dark, 'like an animal', approached them from between the fruit trees and banged loudly on the fence.

On another night, at about 3 a.m., the group heard 'laughter and merriment... which seemed to be coming up the road towards Borley church'. The night was misty, but there was sufficient light to see that nobody was in the roadway. Assuming that the voices were those of late-night revellers, but puzzled by the direction of the sound, Roy Potter got into his car and coasted down the road towards nearby Long Melford with his engine off. He met nobody. Using his walkie-talkie link with Croom-Hollingsworth, he had arranged the experiment of shouting at various points along the Long Melford road to see if the sound carried. The listeners in the churchyard heard nothing. In an attempt to record similar noises, a tape recorder was set up in the porch of the church, while the group kept watch from a distance. Nobody was seen to enter the porch, but the group heard a loud crash and found the tape recorder 'pretty well battered'. The tape had been torn from its reels and lay in a tangle.

But it was the sighting of the nun that convinced the Harlow group that something was indeed strange about Borley. One clear night, Croom-Hollingsworth was standing in the orchard, looking towards the 'nun's walk':

'Suddenly, I saw her quite clearly, in a grey habit and cowl as she moved across the garden and through a hedge. I thought: "Is somebody pulling my leg?" Roy was out in the roadway, and I shouted to him. The figure had disappeared into a modern garage, and I thought that was that; but as Roy joined me, we both saw her come out of the other side. She approached to about 12 feet [3 metres] from us, and we both saw her face, that of an elderly woman in her sixties, perhaps. We followed her as she seemed to glide over a dry ditch as if it wasn't there, before she disappeared into a pile of building bricks. Neither of us was frightened. It was an odd sensation, but peaceful and tranquil.'

Not surprisingly, in view of his experiences, Croom-Hollingsworth had little time for the critics who point to discrepancies in Price's account of the haunting. On the other hand, he said:

'I don't give a damn if Price invented things or not. The basic question is – is the place haunted? And, you can take it from me, it is. I have invented nothing. Roy and I saw the nun quite clearly for a period of about 12 minutes... '

Croom-Hollingsworth's determination impressed Denny Densham, a film director and cameraman. In 1974, he got permission to experiment with tape recorders in the church. The results – which were used by the BBC as a basis for a television programme – are, Densham said, 'quite baffling'.

The first taping began at midnight during the winter months. After the church had been carefully examined and searched, a cassette player was placed by the altar and the investigators sat at the other end of the church. The tape picked up a series of bumps and raps. Next, two tape recorders were locked up in the church, one by the altar and the other halfway down the aisle. Both picked up the unmistakable sound of a heavy door being opened and slammed shut, complete with the squeaking of a bolt. Neither the porch door nor the

WE ALL FELT WATCHED AND A CURIOUS TINGLING SENSATION WAS FELT; ODDLY ENOUGH, THE MACHINES SEEMED TO PICK UP A LOT OF STATIC AT THIS POINT. WE RECORDED STEALTHY SOUNDS NEAR THE ALTAR, THE SOUND OF A DOOR SHUTTING AGAIN, A CRASH AS OF SOMETHING BEING KNOCKED OVER, AND THEN THE SOUND OF HOLLOW, HEAVY FOOTSTEPS...

The Waldegrave tomb, above, is a memorial to an old and influential Borley family. Local gossip had it that the Waldegrave coffins in the vault under the church were mysteriously moved in the 19th century.

One of the stained glass windows of Borley church, right, is dedicated to the Reverend Henry Bull. His retelling of the story of the ghostly nun seen at Borley rectory gave a boost to the reputation of his family home as a haunted house.

smaller chancel door had been opened – the researchers had kept watch on the church from outside – and examination showed that the chancel door bolt did not squeak.

CHURCH VIGIL

The following week, Densham and his team started their vigil at 12.30 a.m. They set up a sophisticated stereo tape with two high quality microphones, again placing one near the altar and the other halfway down the aisle. An additional cassette machine was also positioned in front of the altar. Then half the team were locked into the church and the other half kept watch in the churchyard.

'Suddenly there was a curious change in the atmosphere,' said Densham. 'One of the team felt as if he was being watched, and we all felt very cold.' During the next few minutes, the tapes picked up a clatter, as if something had been thrown down the aisle. There were also knockings, rappings, the sound of the door opening again – although both doors remained locked and bolted – and, chillingly, the sound of a human sigh. Afterwards, the team found that the small cassette recorder had jammed, and the tape had been extracted and tangled up.

In July, the party visited Borley again. At 1.45 a.m., they felt a change in the atmosphere .

'We all felt watched, and a curious tingling sensation was felt; oddly enough, the machines seemed to pick up a lot of static at this point. We recorded stealthy sounds near the altar, the sound of the door shutting again, a crash as of something being knocked over, and then the sound of hollow, heavy footsteps, like those of a very large man walking by the altar rail. We could not reproduce them normally: the floor there is of stone, heavily carpeted.'

The observers then saw a glow of light near the chancel door, followed by a terrifying grunt. On this, their final visit, the team saw pinpoints of light in the curtains by one door, and heard the sound of a heavy crash. Densham said:

'Frankly, I am at a loss to explain what goes on at Borley. We made every effort to ensure that our legs weren't being pulled, and the tapes were new and untampered with. No theory I have tried to put forward seems to pan out. We tried leaving pencil and paper in the church, asked the thing to rap and so on, but it doesn't seem to be trying to communicate, unless the damage to the tapes and the throwing of invisible objects in our direction meant that it resented our presence. One's left with the feeling that whatever causes the phenomena is indifferent to or perhaps unaware of observers.'

After that summer of 1974, one of the most regular researchers at Borley was Ronald R. Russell, a member of the Enfield Parapsychical Research Group and professional photographer. Frank Parry, an electrical engineer, and John Fay, a mechanical engineer, usually worked with him. Russell achieved odd results while taking photographs of the area with an Agfa CC21 camera, in which the film is contained in a cassette and processed in the Agfa laboratory.

'Sandwiched between perfectly normal frames we got "ectoplasmic" stuff in the churchyard, shadows where no shadows should be, and a thin light near the north door. As a photographer, I'm at a loss to explain this as camera or film malfunction.'

The altar in Borley church. is shown, above. In 1974, some strange sounds – including raps, crashes and mysterious footsteps – were picked up here on a cassette recorder.

Frank Parry used a graphic analyser, an eight-channel recording machine with slider controls that adjust pitch and level, cut out interference, and enable its operator to 'pinpoint' sounds. As Ronald R. Russell said:

'We have recorded hundreds of extraordinary noises, footsteps, crashes and so on. On one occasion we located a centre of disturbance near the Waldegrave tomb; it was tangible, like a swirling column of energy. When you passed your hand through it, you felt a sort of crackle, like static electricity. On another occasion, we heard a deep, grunting voice, which reminded me irresistibly of Lee Marvin singing *Wandering Star.*'

The church authorities are non-committal, however, preferring to avoid discussion of the topic. But in the parish guidebook, under the heading 'ghosts', is a footnote:

'There are, of course, those who suggest the church itself is haunted. Many old churches and buildings have noises and chill areas which some would classify as ghostly, but those who have lived long in the village, and we who worship in the church, have not experienced anything which would support such thoughts... Visitors should please remember that this is God's house and treat it with reverence.'

❞ ... THERE SEEMS TO BE SOME SORT OF POWER CONCENTRATED IN THE CHURCH ITSELF... WHEN YOU TRY DOWSING IN THE CHURCH, THE ROD PRACTICALLY TWISTS FROM YOUR HANDS... I WOULD SUGGEST THAT THE POWER IS BOOSTED BY THE PRESENCE OF OBSERVERS... ❞

RONALD R. RUSSELL

VAMPIRES: MYTH AND REALITY

WHATEVER THE TRUTH OF THE VAMPIRE LEGEND, COUNT DRACULA CONTINUES TO HOLD HIS AUDIENCES IN A STATE OF HORRIFIED HALF-BELIEF

In Dracula AD 1972 – a still from which is shown above – Christopher Lee, as the Count, attacks an innocent victim in a typical film interpretation of the vampire legend. The sado-masochistic overtones of the story, with its sexually irresistible attacker and willing victim, contribute to its overwhelming power to fascinate.

In the illustration, above right, three Brahmans make incantations, accompanied by vampires, in a story from Sir Richard Burton's Tales of Hindu Devilry. The tales are purportedly told by the Baital, Indian vampires.

The Day of Judgement, as depicted right, is symbolised by the the struggle to escape from the tomb. In the past, premature burial has all too often been a matter of grim reality.

At the end of the first stage version of *Dracula* in 1924, the actor-manager Hamilton Deane (who played the part of Van Helsing) appeared before the curtain with a little reassurance for the audience:

'Just a moment, ladies and gentlemen! Just a word before you leave. We hope the memories of Dracula.. . won't give you bad dreams, so just a word of reassurance. When you get home tonight and the lights have been turned out and you are afraid to look behind the curtains and you dread to see a face appear at the window – why, pull yourself together! And remember that, after all, *there are such things!*'

It was a perfect exit line. The audience, primed to a fine degree by a background of vampire books, had spent the evening thrilling to the extraordinarily compelling tale of 'the greatest vampire of them all' – Dracula. His creator – the theatre manager, Bram Stoker – knew instinctively that his story would strike some chord deep in the collective subconscious of his audience.

As actor Christopher Lee explained, Dracula appeals partly because he is a superhuman figure, an immortal whose chilling presence is also sexually irresistible. Psychologists point to the clear difference between the sadistic, dominant vampire and the masochistic or subservient victim. But whatever the jargon used, Dracula is generally more fascinating than the atavistic werewolf (who is, after all, at least half animal, and certainly not an aristocrat) or the shadowy ghost.

The vampire is also rather different from 'the creature from the black lagoon' or Dr Who's enemies, the Daleks. Whereas such creatures as these can be dismissed as mere stagecraft, thrilling enough during the performance but forgotten soon after, the vampire is to be taken seriously. Indeed, there are masses of documents from 18th-century Eastern Europe presenting evidence for the existence of the 'undead'. Could it be, then, that there are actually such things?

As in many other aspects of the paranormal, all possible rational explanations must be thoroughly exhausted before a 'supernatural' explanation can even be considered. And in the case of the 'vampire epidemic' of 200 years ago, there are several such rational explanations to choose from.

As the popular occult writer Dennis Wheatley has pointed out, in past times of great deprivation, beggars often broke into graveyards, sleeping in the shelter of mausoleums by day, and emerging at night to forage for food. Thin, pale and seen leaving tombs under cover of darkness, they were, perhaps not unnaturally, often taken for the legendary and terrifying vampires.

However, the mistaken identity of a few human scavengers does not explain those cases of corpses found to be incorrupt when their coffins were opened. This is a rare but by no means unknown phenomenon and various 'natural' explanations have been suggested as the cause of it. Certainly, the soil in which a body is buried can make an astonishing difference to the rate at which it decomposes. On the volcanic island of Santorini, Greece, for example, corpses are sometimes found so intact after a great number of years that the local people have a saying that speaks of 'sending a vampire to Santorini', just as the British might speak of 'sending coals to Newcastle' – that is, sending goods to a region where they are superfluous.

But by far the most convincing explanation is that of premature burial. Not all cataleptics were as fortunate as the Irish soldier, in the early 1800s, who 'came back to life' when being roughly handled prior to his burial. Coma, catalepsy and other death-like states are barely understood by the modern world, let alone by superstitious peasants from 'the land beyond the forests' in times gone by.

Indeeed, how many poor wretches may have awoken to discover themselves immured in a coffin with the heavy earth pressing down on them; or perhaps, having successfully fought their way out of the coffin, found themselves locked in the family mausoleum, there to die of hunger, thirst and inevitable horror?

TERROR BEYOND THE GRAVE

Premature burial was, in fact, common. It is even said that, when an 18th-century English graveyard was being demolished to make way for a car park, a third of the corpses turned up by the bulldozer showed signs of having struggled while in their coffins. The evidence included broken fingers from scratching at the coffin lid in their final death agony, hands protruding from the coffin, and blood upon the shroud where the 'corpse' had bitten his or her own flesh as suffocation, or madness, took its toll. Indeed, it was the presence of blood on an exhumed corpse that was frequently considered proof that the dead person was a vampire.

But if the newly dead was rumoured to be a vampire (perhaps feeble sounds may have been heard emanating from the grave), then the terrified 'witnesses' would take the time-honoured measures against it. And if the 'corpse's' heart was beating, that was, to them, a sure sign that it must be staked. No wonder there are so many accounts of alleged vampires screaming as the stake was plunged into their living hearts.

Charlotte Stoker used to tell the young Bram a grisly bedtime story concerning a local victim of the cholera epidemic. This woman, believed dead, was thrown on the heap of corpses in the lime pit. However, her grief-stricken husband, who went to recover her body in order to give her a decent burial, discovered she was still breathing. She lived on happily for many years after that appalling experience. But what if she had recovered by herself and had been seen staggering out of the pit at night? It would have been easy to mistake her for one of the 'undead'.

From time to time, modern newspapers carry stories of people, certified dead, coming to life on the marble slab in the morgue or when being prepared for burial. In these days of 'spare part' surgery, controversy rages over the exact moment and true nature of death more than at any point in history. But the Victorians were at least aware of the possibility of premature burial; some even became obsessed with the idea. Edgar Allan Poe based several of his stories on the theme; and in both the United States and Europe, various patents were taken out on coffins with alarm bells or emergency air supplies incorporated into their design.

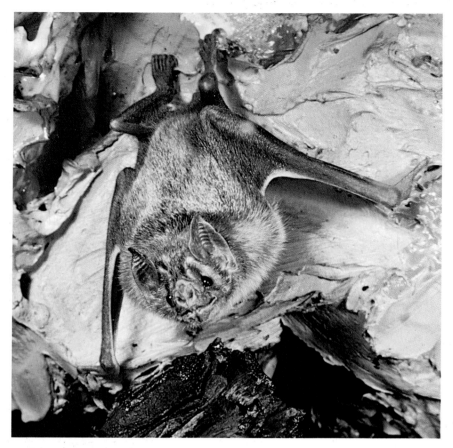

There is even a logical explanation for the widespread use of garlic as a vampire repellent. Plague was frequently carried by flies, and it was noticed that certain farms were spared if they hung out garlic. There was no magic involved; garlic bulbs exude drops of moisture that flies detest. Garlic, when eaten, is also believed to be a natural antiseptic, and a blood purifier.

Vampires were also a useful scapegoat in certain rural communities, if animals weakened and died. These days, the vet would no doubt administer a dose of antibiotics or special vitamin supplement and all would be well – in most cases. Mysterious sicknesses and mutilations of cattle and other animals do still sometimes occur; but in some regions, hostile ufonauts are now occasionally deemed to be the culprits.

DEMONIC BLOODSUCKERS

There may frequently be logical, even mundane, explanations for 99 out of every 100 cases of alleged vampirism, but it is the hundredth case that will set the researcher wondering. For many years, occultists have believed in the terrifying existence of demonic bloodsucking materialisations. One, the practising occultist Dion Fortune (whose real name was Violet Firth), believed that it is possible for the 'astral body' to escape from a person's living body and assume another form such as a bird, an animal – or a vampire.

Dion Fortune also cited the case of dead Hungarian soldiers who are believed to have become vampires during the First World War, maintaining themselves in the 'etheric double' – that is, halfway between this world and the next, or 'earthbound' – by vampirising the wounded. Vampirism is, indeed, believed to be contagious; and the person who is vampirised, being depleted of vitality, is thought to be a turned into a psychic vacuum, capable of absorbing the 'life force' from anyone unfortunate enough to fall prey to him.

Psychical research, on the other hand, deals not with beliefs but with observed facts. One of the most common of all phenomena investigated by the Society for Psychical Research in London, for example, is that of the poltergeist; and an allied phenomenon seems to be that of the invisible attacker. Raised scratch marks appeared on the face of poltergeist victim Eleonore Zugun of Rumania, during 1926, for example. And, in 1960, Jimmy de Bruin, a 20-year-old farm worker in South Africa, became the focus for a spate of poltergeist activity. On one occasion, an investigating police officer actually heard de Bruin scream with agony as cuts spontaneously appeared on his legs and chest.

Other areas of the paranormal also involve the spontaneous appearance of wounds or blood, such as images that are suddenly observed to bleed and individuals who produce stigmata. These. however, are commonly accepted as 'holy' phenomena, whereas vampirism is widely believed to be 'of the Devil'. It may indeed be true that they are opposite sides of the same coin, one good and the other evil. But perhaps all unexplained phenomena emanate from the same source, being neither moral nor immoral, just unusual. Meanwhile, we can continue to thrill to the latest vampire tale and ponder on the nature of its origin.

Premature burial may often have arisen because the various steps of *rigor mortis* are commonly misunderstood. The muscles of a corpse start to go rigid, beginning in the face and neck, about an hour-and-a-half after death. (This may set in sooner or later, depending on the temperature of the surroundings.) *Rigor mortis* passes off roughly 36 hours later – the muscles lose their extreme rigidity and the body becomes relatively pliable. This could well be the explanation for the 'vampire' story heard in 1974 in the valley of Curtea de Arges, Rumania. Here, a handsome gypsy woman described, through an interpreter, the shock of her family when they came to lay out her father's body for burial; for the limbs were pliable, not rigid. This news raced through the village, where this could mean only one thing – the old man had become a vampire. A stake was duly plunged through his heart, and the villagers were satisfied and relieved. But perhaps – if this was not simply a case of *rigor mortis* passing off prematurely – the old man was still alive.

*The vampire bat, **Desmodus rotundus, above, is found in Mexico and South America. These creatures, only about 3 inches (8 centimetres) long, are able to feed on the blood of sleeping animals without awakening them.***

▮▮ VAMPIRISM IS BELIEVED TO BE CONTAGIOUS; AND THE PERSON WHO IS VAMPIRISED, BEING DEPLETED OF VITALITY, IS THOUGHT TO BE TURNED INTO A PSYCHIC VACUUM... ▮▮

GHOST MONITOR

In the late 20th century, the search for ghosts has taken a sharply technological turn. Robin Laurence leads one of Britain's most active ghost-hunting units and employs some of the latest equipment to monitor the presence of spirits

E ver since I was a child, I've been interested in the paranormal and ghosts. As a schoolboy, I definitely experienced a few strange things. For example, one day while playing at a friend's house, we happened to hear banging and crashing from next door. We were quite concerned because we knew the neighbours were out. Later, when they were told about the noises, they said: 'Don't worry about it, it's only the ghost.' Apparently, these sounds were heard in the house all the time.

It was because of this deep interest in the paranormal that, in 1987, I formed the Thanet Psychic & Paranormal Research Unit. My aim was to try and make it easier to investigate hauntings. Obviously, as an ordinary person, you can't knock on somebody's door and say: 'Can I come in and have a look at your ghost?' It is easier to do so, however, as part of an 'official' body.

There are other, larger, groups with similar interests, such as the Ghost Club (of which I am an ex-member) and the Society for Psychical Research, but members tend to sit around and wait for cases to come along. I like to get out and find cases to investigate.

At the moment, we are looking into historic sites - trying to find out if they actually do have ghosts. Last year, we investigated about four or five places. Of those, the best was a famous castle in southern England where there have been at least six separate sightings over the past three years. One was of a 17th-century pikeman, who apparently walked into the guardroom through one wall and out again through another. But the most common report is the sound of banging doors - doors that are not there any more!

Our chief methods of investigation are all-night vigils, and the use of certain detecting equipment. In the case of this castle, we had audio tape and video cameras set up at certain spots in the underground tunnels. Sixteen members of the Unit - including myself - broke up into teams to cover different areas.

At 5.20 a.m., one of the cameras recorded the solid double doors on the second floor of the keep

At a strategic spot in the tunnels of Fort Amherst, Robin Laurence sets up the computer's base unit for monitoring the presence of any ghosts.

being vigorously shaken by something unseen. It lasted for about six seconds and there was no natural explanation for it. I myself heard the loud noises, and ran down with others to see what was happening. That film is undoubtedly the most impressive evidence we have for ghost – or, I should say, poltergeist – activity.

I am not at all psychic. I regard myself as an ordinary person, with no extra powers. So it is mainly from a scientific point of view that we undertake these investigations - to prove that these things exist.

> **"** ...IT IS MAINLY FROM A
> SCIENTIFIC POINT OF VIEW THAT
> WE UNDERTAKE THESE
> INVESTIGATIONS... **"**

For each vigil, we take along some basic equipment - torches, notebooks, pens, tape recorder, camera with flash facility, and the video equipment. But we have also been using a computer system, which consists of a lap-top computer linked to a base unit. This picks up signals from individual sensors - placed at strategic points - which detect movement and any drop in temperature (a phenomenon that is frequently associated with the presence of a ghost). The computer records where anything happens, and the time it occurs.

We used the computer system for our vigil at Rochester Castle and also for our most recent investigation - at Fort Amherst, a Napoleonic fortress overlooking Chatham in Kent, which has a vast underground tunnel network. We chose Fort Amherst because they run a ghost tour on Friday evenings, and I thought it might be useful to find out whether there is any truth behind the stories they tell. In fact, I discovered that workmen on the site have reported being physically pushed aside by an invisible force and hearing footsteps in the tunnels on many occasions.

We set up our equipment in the fort's tunnels, though the lights were on. Lights do not, it seems, affect ghosts; we get reports of ghosts being seen at all times of the day. Unfortunately, we did not pick up anything on the computer. Nothing broke the infra-red beam that would record a passing spirit; nor did the temperature drop.

Still, I have been convinced of the existence of ghosts for a long time. What they are, I'm not sure. My favourite explanation is the 'stone-tape' theory, which says that an image can be stored within the fabric of a building, rather like a video recording. So if the conditions are right, a scene that happened 200 years ago can replay.

These days, most of my spare time is taken up with ghost-hunting. I am sure we are going to get some really positive results in the next few years. Ideally, I would like to see a ghost on a video, perhaps walking through a wall. That would be the ultimate thing.

GHOSTS WITHOUT SOULS

IF GHOSTS ARE SPIRITS OF THE DEAD, AS MANY BELIEVE, HOW CAN WE ACCOUNT FOR WHAT SEEM TO BE 'SOULLESS' APPARITIONS – THOSE OF ANIMALS AND INANIMATE OBJECTS?

During the 1930s, a large red London bus on a number 7 route was known to harass motorists in the North Kensington area late at night. The junction of St Mark's Road and Cambridge Gardens had long been considered a dangerous corner: in fact, the bend was 'blind' from both roads and had caused numerous accidents.

The decision of the local authority to straighten out the bend was partially influenced by the testimony of late-night motorists, who said that they had crashed while swerving to avoid a double-decker that was hurtling down St Mark's Road in the small hours, long after regular buses had ceased service.

A typical report to the Kensington police read: 'I was turning the corner and saw a bus tearing towards me. The lights of the top and bottom decks were full on, as were the headlights, but I could see no sign of crew or passengers. I yanked my steering wheel hard over, and mounted the pavement, scraping the roadside wall. The bus just vanished.'

After one fatal accident, during which a driver had swerved and hit the wall, an eyewitness told the coroner's inquest that he, too, had seen the mystery bus hurtling towards the car seconds before the driver spun off the road. When the coroner expressed what was perhaps natural cynicism,

The story of the phantom ship, right, was reported by the American minister and author Dr Cotton Mather in his book Wonders of the Invisible World. *The ship set sail from America but never reached its destination in England and nothing was ever heard of it again. Some months later, however, spectators at the port from which it had sailed witnessed what seemed to be the very same ship, appearing in a cloud. It was seen to keel over and then simply disappeared.*

The junction of St Mark's Road and Cambridge Gardens in Kensington, London, became renowned in the 1930s for the mysterious double-decker bus, like the one shown below, which travelled at great speed in that area in the middle of the night – when there was no public transport.

dozens of local residents wrote to his office and also to the local newspapers, offering to testify that they had seen the 'ghost bus' as well. Among the most impressive of these witnesses was a local transport official who claimed that he had seen the vehicle draw up to the bus depot in the early hours of the morning, stand with engine purring for a moment, and then disappear.

The mystery was never solved; but it is perhaps significant that the 'ghost' bus was not seen after the danger of the sharp corner was removed. It was even suggested that the vision had been 'projected' on to the spot to dramatise the inherent danger of the intersection. But if so, by whom? And if, as was also suggested, this all took place in the minds of the motorists themselves – a sort of natural projection of their fears at the corner – how did they manage to superimpose it on the vision of the passersby, not to mention the bus depot official who saw it all from an entirely different angle?

The phantom bus of Kensington epitomises a problem that, for centuries, has faced those who believe that ghosts are revenant spirits. If a ghost is

'Ghostly' lore is strewn with stories of all sorts of inanimate objects suddenly becoming apparent – everything from the 'phantom' accordion accredited to Daniel Dunglas Home, the 19th-century Spiritualist, to Macbeth's dagger. In the latter case, William Shakespeare, writing in an age steeped in superstition, seems to have been as aware of the anomaly of 'spirit objects' as he was of almost every other field of human experience: '. . . art thou, O fateful dagger, sensible to feeling as to sight, or art thou but a dagger of the mind, a false creation, proceeding from the heat oppressed brain?'

HOVERING SHAPE

One of the most convincing stories of totally 'soul-less' apparitions is recorded in the day book of the Tower of London – a place that, according to popular belief, is saturated with ghosts. The man who made the entry was named Edmund Lenthal Swifte. In 1814, he was appointed Keeper of the Crown Jewels, and continued in the office until 1842 – a total of 28 years. The account of what Swifte saw on a Sunday evening in October 1817 is best left to him:

'I was at supper with my wife, our little boy, and my wife's sister in the sitting room of the Jewel House, which is said to have been the "doleful prison" of Anne Boleyn and of the ten bishops whom Oliver Cromwell piously accommodated there. The doors were all closed, heavy and dark curtains were let down over the windows, and the only light in the room was that of two candles on the table. I sat at the foot of the table, my son on my right, my wife fronting the chimney piece, and her sister on the opposite side. I had offered a glass of wine and water to my wife when, on putting it to her lips, she paused, and exclaimed, "Good God! what is that?"

'I looked up, and saw a cylindrical figure, like a glass tube, something about the thickness of my arm, and hovering between the ceiling and table; its contents appeared to be a dense fluid, white and pale azure . . . incessantly rolling and mingling within the cylinder. This lasted about two minutes, when it began to move before my sister-in-law, following the oblong shape of the table, before my son and myself. Passing behind my wife, it paused for a moment over her right shoulder (observe, there was no mirror opposite in which she could then behold it.) Instantly, she crouched down, and with both hands covering her shoulder, shrieked out: "Oh Christ! It has seized me!"

'Even now as I write, I feel the horror of that moment. I caught up my chair, striking at the appearance with a blow that hit the wainscot behind her. It then crossed the upper end of the table and disappeared in the recess of the opposite window.'

There was no recurrence of this curious manifestation; but some years later, it did help Swifte's judgement of a soldier in the Tower who actually died from fright, brought on by what he had seen outside Swifte's front door.

The soldier had been on guard outside the Jewel House when, at around midnight, he had heard a guttural snarl behind him and turned to see a huge black bear, reared up on its hind legs, fangs bared, eyes red with rage, and talons groping towards him.

In his book Supernature, *Lyall Watson, below, suggests that the fact that ghosts appear as people remember them indicates that apparitions are part of a mental process rather than a supernatural one. Certainly, most ghosts do appear fully clothed or are dressed in a shroudlike garment, as was the ghost that terrorised the residents of Hammersmith, London, in the early 1800s,* bottom.

the 'soul' of a dead person returned to earth, how do we account for phantom buses – and, of course, their lineal ancestors, phantom coaches, which feature so heavily in folklore?

Come to that, why do returning spirits not appear in the nude – for, with very few reliably recorded exceptions, none do?

❚❚ ALL THE GHOSTS OF WHICH I HAVE EVER HEARD WORE CLOTHES. WHILE I AM PREPARED IN PRINCIPLE TO CONCEDE THE POSSIBILITY OF AN ASTRAL BODY, I CANNOT BRING MYSELF TO BELIEVE IN ASTRAL SHOES AND SHIRTS AND HATS. ❚❚

LYALL WATSON, SUPERNATURE

ACTIVE IMAGINATION

CASEBOOK

The eminent Swiss psychologist Carl Jung (1875-1961) was deeply interested in many aspects of the paranormal, and keenly recorded his own experiences in this area, as well as following with active enthusiasm discoveries being made by parapsychologists during his lifetime.

One of the most intriguing events to occur to him personally took place during a trip to Ravenna, Italy, with a friend. Here, he was particularly struck by a mosaic that depicted Christ extending his hand to Peter as the disciple appeared to be drowning at sea. Both Jung and his companion apparently looked closely at the mosaic for many minutes and talked in some detail about it. Deeply struck by its imagery and design, Jung had wanted to buy a reproduction of the work but had no luck in finding one.

On his return home, Jung learned that another friend was about to visit Ravenna and so asked whether a photograph could be taken of the favourite mosaic. Strangely, however, it was discovered that no such mosaic had ever existed at Ravenna. The mosaic must therefore have been, Jung was bound to concede, a shared apparition – and one of the most extraordinary experiences of his life.

This bizarre occurrence seems in many ways to relate to what Jung had termed 'active imagination' – a technique that he is known to have taught to some of his patients. In 1935, during a series of lectures given at London's Tavistock Clinic, he described how a young artist he knew was able to project himself into an alpine landscape that was depicted on a poster, even to the extent of walking over the hill that it featured and viewing a fantasy chapel that he was convinced lay beyond.

The soldier rammed his bayonet into the belly of the animal, but the weapon passed clean through and the apparition disappeared.

A patrol found the soldier a few moments later, as he lay senseless. The bayonet, with a heavy 'Tower issue' musket attached, was embedded in the solid wood of the door. The soldier was taken, still insensible, to the guardroom, where a doctor pronounced that he was neither drunk nor asleep. The following morning, Swifte interviewed him; over and over, the soldier repeated his bizarre tale until, three days later, he died.

For about 300 years, until the middle of the 17th century, the Tower of London housed a royal menagerie, and among the animals recorded as having been kept there were a number of bears. Although no account of an autopsy on the soldier survives, the fact that he died three days after his experience could indicate that he was seriously ill without knowing it, and that the apparition was an

Phantom horses, as depicted below, complete with riders, are a common form of haunting and are usually associated with a particular place. According to one theory, they are a kind of recording of a highly emotional or dramatic event which is 'replayed' in certain circumstances.

hallucination caused by his condition. On the other hand, animal ghosts make more sense as 'revenant spirits' than their human counterparts: they at least 'appear' exactly as in life. The fact that Man has lost most of his 'primitive' instincts, while animals retain theirs, may also have an as-yet unexplained bearing on such instances.

PHANTOM BEASTS

Stories of phantom dogs are common to the United States, Europe, and many parts of Africa. Ghostly horses, cattle, and even sheep have their part in folklore, too; and although, like all folk tales, accounts of their appearances have undoubtedly become distorted in the telling over centuries, some are eerily convincing. In 1908, the British Society for Psychical Research (SPR) made exhaustive enquiries into the appearance of what appeared to be a phantom pig in the village of Hoe Benham, near Newbury, Berkshire.

On 2 November 1907, two young men named Oswald Pittman and Reginald Waud were painting in the garden of their house, Laburnum Villa. At around 10 a.m., Pittman got up to speak to the milkman and saw his friend, Clarissa Miles, coming up the lane: she was due to join the men for a painting session. Accompanying her, like a pet dog, was a large white pig with an unusually long snout. When Pittman told Waud about it, Waud asked him to tell Clarissa to keep the animal outside and close the garden gate securely, as Waud was a keen gardener and did not want the pig wandering among his plants.

However, when Clarissa arrived, she was alone, and denied all knowledge of the animal. If it had been following her, she pointed out, she would surely have heard its steps. Nevertheless, she and Pittman went back up the lane and asked several children if they had seen a pig that day, but none of them had.

The following morning, the milkman, pressed by a bewildered Pittman, signed a statement to the effect that he had not seen the pig, and pointed out

that, in any case, the area was under a swine fever curfew, and any stray animal would be destroyed.

Pittman and Waud went to London for few months and, while there, reported the odd incident to a member of the SPR. By the time they returned to Hoe Benham in February, the story of Pittman's apparition had become widespread. Shedding their natural reserve, the villagers inundated them with stories of previous 'phantoms'. Local theory had it that they all stemmed from the suicide of a certain farmer, Tommy King, whose estate, which was demolished in 1892, had bordered the lane. Investigation of the parish records showed there had in fact been two Tommy Kings, one dying in 1741 and the other in 1753, but there was no indication of which one had committed suicide. An old man named John Barrett testified that, when he was a boy in 1850, he had been returning with seven or eight others in a hay cart along the lane when 'a white thing' appeared in the air. All the men had seen it, and the horses obviously had, too, for they suddenly went wild.

'This thing kept a-bobbin' and a-bobbin' and the horses kept a-snortin' and a-snortin' until the wagon reached the neighbourhood of King's Farm, when the shape vanished.' In 1873, at the same spot, Barrett had also seen a creature 'like a sheep' pawing the ground in the lane. He tried to take a blow at it with his stick, but it disappeared before the stick landed.

Another man, Albert Thorne, said that, in the autumn of 1904, he had heard 'a noise like a whizzin' of leaves, and saw summat like a calf knuckled down' about 221 feet (75 centimetres) high and 5 feet (1.5 metres) long, with glowing eyes. As he watched, it faded away. Yet another witness, unnamed, said that, in bright moonlight during January 1905, he had seen what he took to be the curate's dog in the lane. It was large and black. Assuming that it had strayed, he went to grab it, whereupon it appeared to turn into a donkey, rising up on its hind legs threateningly before vanishing.

UNEARTHLY SCREAM

Pittman, Waud, and Clarissa Miles reported one more unnerving experience. Once, while walking in the lane, Clarissa was suddenly overcome by an irrational fear, and told her companions that she felt the presence of an evil being, charged with malice towards them. She also felt that she was suffocating. As they reached the spot where Pittman had seen the pig, all three heard an 'unearthly scream', although no one else was about. Waud, who had been sceptical from the start, was finally convinced by this strange and terrible cry that the ghostly animal existed.

The sensitivity of animals, particularly cats and dogs, to paranormal phenomena is almost a truism. Dr Robert Morris, a parapsychologist who has used animals as 'controls' in his experiments, tells of a particular investigation of a haunted house, in one room of which a tragedy had occurred. He used a dog, cat, rat, and rattlesnake.

'The dog, upon being taken about two or three feet [less than a metre] into the room, immediately snarled at its owner and backed out of the door. No amount of cajoling could prevent the dog from

Legend has it that a 17th-century phantom coach, constructed of the bones of the four husbands of the wicked Lady Howard – all of whom she is said to have murdered – travels the road that runs across the moor from Tavistock to near Okehampton Castle, shown below. The sheeted spectre of Lady Howard rides inside the coach and a skeleton-hound runs before it. According to the legend, each night the hound must pick a blade of grass from Okehampton Park to take back to Lady Howard's family home at Tavistock – a penance to be endured until every blade of grass has finally been picked.

struggling to get out and it refused to re-enter. The cat was brought into the room, carried in its owner's arms. When the cat got a similar distance into the room, it immediately leaped upon the owner's shoulders, dug in, then leaped to the ground, orienting itself towards a chair. It spent several minutes hissing and spitting and staring at the unoccupied chair in a corner of the room until it was finally removed,' Morris reports.

The rattlesnake then immediately assumed an attack posture, focusing on the same chair that had been of interest to the cat. After a couple of minutes, it slowly moved its head toward a window, moved back and then receded into its alert posture about five minutes later.

The rat was the only creature not to react at all on that occasion, but all four animals were tested in a separate room some time later, and there behaved perfectly normally.

In the misty world of apparitions, no one – not even the most dedicated psychical researcher – knows quite what is the motivation behind them. What we *do* know is that they are not confined to human beings: the ghosts of both animals and inanimate objects – even the 'soul' of a London bus – have been lucidly recorded by many perplexed witnesses over the years.

ANOTHER SCOTTISH HAUNTING

WHY DOES THE GHOST OF THE WRETCHED ALEXANDER GILLAN LINGER AT THE SITE OF HIS EXECUTION ON A LONELY SCOTTISH MOOR? WAS HE INNOCENT OF THE MURDER FOR WHICH HE WAS IGNOMINIOUSLY HANGED?

The Muir of Stynie, below, is the lonely moor, shunned by locals for fear of the ghost of murderer Alexander Gillan. Charles Hope, Lord Justice Clerk to the Scottish Sessions, right, was the judge who convicted Gillan. A man of imposing presence with a magnificent voice and a gift for declamation, Hope had the reputation of being brutally harsh to felons.

The low-lying coast of Grampian, around the mouth of Scotland's River Spey, has always been a bleak and desolate place, a natural breeding ground for stories of the supernatural. There is, according to local legend, a black dog with 'eyes like cogies' (whisky tumblers) that prowls through the local forests; a Red Fisherman is said to foretell death; and it is widely believed that the 'Auld Guidman', once the local landlord, still guards

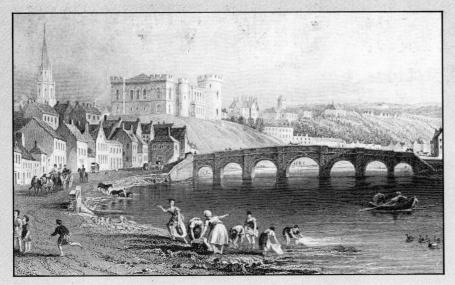

the Bog of Gight with a medieval claymore (two-edged broadsword).

But the best known story, as convincing now as it was 170 years ago, is of the ghost of Alexander Gillan, said to stalk the Muir of Stynie. Apparently, even Crown Forestry workers and gamekeepers avoid this area at night for fear of meeting his ghost on a cart track known as 'Gillan's Way'.

Alexander Gillan was a farm labourer who lived alone in the hamlet of Lhanbryde, a few miles east of Elgin. One account has it that he was an Irish immigrant and distrusted by his neighbours; another, that he was a half-witted orphan. One misty night in August 1810, a 10-year-old girl – named

It was at Inverness, above, that Alexander Gillan stood trial. After being convicted, he was kept in its pestilential Tolbooth jail on a diet of bread and water until, on the day of his execution, he was thrown into a cart and taken to the scene of his crime to be hanged.

Elspet Lamb – disappeared while she was walking from her father's croft at Lhanbryde to the hamlet of Urquhart, 2 miles (3 kilometres) away. The next morning, men-at-arms from Elgin searched the surrounding moors and forests while prayers were offered in the local kirk for her safety. Alexander Gillan was present in the congregation. The hunters used tracker dogs and soon found the girl's body in a thicket on the Muir of Stynie, 'her head battered open', as they described it.

A pair of blood-stained trousers was found in a nearby trench. Locals quickly identified them as belonging to Alexander Gillan. He was arrested just as the kirk service finished, wearing his 'best breeks' (trousers). He was charged with 'molesting' and murdering Elspet Lamb, and taken to Inverness to be tried. The date for the trial was fixed for 29 September 1810.

Gillan, unfortunately, appeared before Charles Hope, Lord Justice Clerk to the Scottish Sessions. Hope was a self-made man, who had risen from being a poor law student to Member of Parliament for Edinburgh. He was a high Tory, thought by many to be a disciplinarian and a snob, who had nevertheless endeared himself to the Scottish gentry by his 'integrity, kindness and gentleman-like manners'. However, when sitting as a judge, he seemed to abandon these qualities and could be brutally harsh with those appearing before him. His judicial contemporary, Lord Cockburn, described him as being 'greatly wanting in tact and judgement'.

According to the Inverness records, the case against Gillan was considered watertight, even though the trousers were not positively identified as being his, and though he was not questioned as

to his whereabouts on the night of the crime.

At the trial, he clutched a crumpled piece of paper from which he attempted to read, but he was not given any opportunity to speak in his own defence. Instead, with the black cap lying beside him, Hope launched into a 10-minute declamation that must be one of the most spine-chilling judgements ever handed out.

'I look upon any punishment you can receive in this world as mercy. Did you flatter yourself that if you escaped detection and conviction, you could have lived and taken your place amongst the decent-living and industrious, amidst the daily avocations [occupations] of your fellow men?

'The mangled corpse of this innocent child would have unceasingly haunted you. Her departed spirit would have drawn aside your curtain at midnight, and horror and remorse and despair would surely have driven you, at length, to take vengeance upon yourself.'

Even God found crimes such as Gillan's hard to forgive, said the judge, particularly as:

'... It was no small aggravation of your foul deed that you went reeking with the blood of your victim to The Temple of the Lord, impiously to mix with God-fearing people while they offered up their prayers. You thought that by going to Church, assuming the solemn appearance and devout conduct of Christian people, you would be able to conceal your guilt, but you lost that composure which a conscience at ease bestows... so the House of God, to which you had impiously fled to cover your wickedness, became a means of bringing your guilt to the light of day.'

Bereft of Burial

The Lord Justice Clerk ordered pastors to attend Gillan during his last days in order that he might prepare himself for death.

'But it is decreed that a criminal such as you shall be bereft of all burial and that his body shall not be permitted to descend into its Mother Earth like those of Christians. I have resolved to make you a lasting and memorable example of the fate which awaits the commission of such deeds as yours.

> ❝ THERE ARE APPARITIONS OF
> SOULS WHICH DEPARTED FROM
> THE BODY IN A STATE OF IMPURITY,
> AND STILL PARTAKE OF
> CORRUPTION AND THE VISIBLE
> WORLD, AND THEREFORE ARE
> LIABLE TO BE SEEN. THESE ARE
> NOT THE SOULS OF GOOD MEN
> BUT OF BAD... ❞
>
> **SOCRATES**

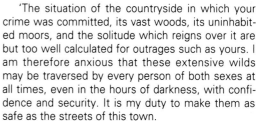

At the 'red kirk' of Lhanbryde, above, men-at-arms arrested Gillan as he was leaving after the service.

Henry Gordon, seventh Duke of Richmond (1845-1928), below, agreed, in 1911, that Gillan's gibbet was a public nuisance and should be taken down and buried where it stood. When a hole was dug, the remains of a human skeleton were discovered.

'The situation of the countryside in which your crime was committed, its vast woods, its uninhabited moors, and the solitude which reigns over it are but too well calculated for outrages such as yours. I am therefore anxious that these extensive wilds may be traversed by every person of both sexes at all times, even in the hours of darkness, with confidence and security. It is my duty to make them as safe as the streets of this town.

'I have therefore determined that, after your execution, you shall be hung suspended in chains until the birds of the air pick the flesh off your body, and your bones bleach and moulder in the winds of heaven, thereby to afford a continuing warning of the consequences of doing as you did and operating, I hope, as an example for the prevention of such crimes, and for procuring the safety of all people proceeding around the region. Therefore you shall be taken from the prison and, on some convenient part of the moor near to the place where the crime was committed, be hanged by the neck until you are dead. This I pronounce for doom. And may God Almighty have mercy on your soul.'

On the morning of Wednesday, 14 November, Alexander Gillan, weak from a diet of bread and water only, was driven the 40 miles (64 kilometres) south to the Muir of Stynie in a cart. There, in the dying winter light, a 12-foot (3.6-metre) high oaken gallows had been erected; beside it, on the ground, lay what the *Huntly Express* described as 'an ingenious device, a cage of bands and chains and swivels.'

Gillan had had no opportunity to speak out at his trial, nor did he have one now. Still clutching a piece of paper, he was bundled up the ladder by a hangman and, 'the noose being tightened around his neck, he was swung off into eternity with the piece of paper from which he had intended to read the statement of his sorrow and repentance.'

As soon as he was dead, the body was taken down and shackled into the iron cage; then, this was hoisted up and hung from the gallows. The officials withdrew down a rutted track, which quickly became known as 'Gillan's Way'.

However, at dawn the following morning, the body had gone, though the cage was still there. The men-at-arms questioned local villagers at Lhanbryde, Urquhart and Garmouth, but nobody divulged anything.

In spite of this, the gallows and empty cage were left where they were. Charles Hope died 41 years later in 1851, but the gallows were to outlast him by 60 years. The solid oak, swivels and rusting chains withstood the corrosive sea mists 'becoming', according to the *Northern Scot* newspaper, 'a nuisance to those living nearby. In the gentlest breezes, the ironwork rattled and groaned, but in a gale the swivels spun and squealed and were heard for miles downwind.'

Quite soon, people reported a different kind of nuisance. Those who had been down Gillan's Way said they had seen the shadowy figure of Alexander Gillan lurking beneath the pine trees. For weeks after his death, people said that the scrap of paper that he had been clutching had been seen blowing about beneath the gallows. But no one dared pick it up and read it.

The cross that marks Gillan's grave, below, is said to have been made from an arm of the gallows on which he was hanged. It has weathered the years remarkably well. A strong iron rivet was driven through its centre, presumably in accordance with the tradition that iron stakes keep the unhallowed dead from 'walking'. But the locals still avoid the area of 'Gillan's Way', especially after dark.

One hundred and one years after the hanging, the then Duke of Richmond agreed that 'Gillan's gibbet' was a public nuisance and he ordered it to be taken down and buried at that very spot. While a trench was being dug, human bones were unearthed. The Duke was immediately told and he went, with a local doctor, to investigate. The doctor identified one of the bones as a man's thigh bone. The remaining bones were left where they were. Obviously, almost immediately after the hanging, someone had lowered the cage, taken Gillan out and buried him there and then. The Duke had the bones replaced, the gallows laid on top of them and the trench filled in. Later, a cross (reputedly made from the arm of the gallows, presumably by a local) was erected on the spot.

The cross is still there, though very few people, even locals, know its exact location. It is made of rock-hard, weathered oak, and has a great iron rivet driven through its centre.

One person who knows its whereabouts said:

'My grandmother was one of the folks who petitioned the Duke to pull the gallows down. Our family was closest to the site, and never a day nor a night went by without the sound of the gibbet stirring. I remember, as a child, myself and some friends tried to put flowers on the grave in the summer, and a keeper caught us at it. He was angry; he said that it was unhallowed ground, and no good would come of laying flowers there as you would on a Christian grave. And what do I feel about it? I rarely come here. I'll drive my tractor along Gillan's Way to the pub at dinner time, but at night I take the long way round. It depresses you. The area carries a black depression about it, especially at dusk.'

The Muir of Stynie is looked after by the Forestry Commission. Land officers treat the story with respect. As one of them puts it: 'I'm not a local but the place worries me simply because you never see deer or a bird there: a hundred yards [30 metres] away, yes, but that place is always deserted.'

One interesting point about this ghost story is that most accounts tally in almost every respect. One version, however, goes further than the rest:

" HE GOT THE WRONG LASSIE. HE WAS NO' A BAD MAN, BY ALL ACCOUNTS, BUT HE'D FALLEN FOR ELSPET'S ELDER SISTER AND SHE'D JILTED HIM. SO HE WAITED FOR HER BY THE FOREST SIDE THERE, AND HE GOT THE WRONG ONE IN THE MIST. THAT'S WHAT WAS WRITTEN ON THE SCRAP OF PAPER, AND SOME AROUND HERE KNEW IT. SO THEY TOOK HIM DOWN AND THEY BURIED HIM, IN SPITE OF THE HIGH JUDGE. **"**

POLTERGEISTS, UNLIKE GHOSTS, 'HAUNT' BY CAUSING COMMOTIONS, MAKING NOISES, THROWING THINGS AROUND AND CREATING CHAOS. ARE THEY MALEVOLENT SPIRITS, OR MERELY PROJECTIONS, PERHAPS, OF THE UNCONSCIOUS MIND?

Mysterious bangs, loud crashes, objectionable smells and furniture that moves about on its own; sudden cold spells, inexplicable voices, objects that appear and disappear, and the uncontrolled levitation of victims – these are all symptoms of poltergeist activity. (The word poltergeist is derived from two German words – a folklore term, *polter,* meaning 'noisy' and the word for spirit, *geist*). The development of psychical research and parapsychology during the last 100 years has also introduced into the language a more cumbersome phrase sometimes used to describe the same phenomena – recurrent spontaneous psychokinesis (or RSPK).

EVIL FORCES?

Such disturbances have been recorded since at least the 12th century. At one time, they were believed to be caused by mysterious, evil forces. Writing in the 13th century, a Welshman, for instance, noted that a 'spirit' was heard to converse with a group of men in a most alarming fashion. But it was not until 300 years later, in 1599, that one of the first authentic examinations of this type of incident was undertaken by Martin del Rio. He described 18 kinds of demon, including one that seemed to specialise in causing disturbances:

SPIRITS
ON THE RAMPAGE

In May 1985, teacher Ken Webster experienced violent poltergeist activity at his cottage in the village of Dodleston, near Chester. Much of the disturbance centred on the kitchen, left, where furniture was upended and small items thrown about.

PERSPECTIVES

THE PHANTOM FACE

Poltergeists, it seems, sometimes haunt commercial premises as well as invading the home. In 1973, Manfred Cassirer – member of the council of Britain's Society for Psychical Research – was called in to investigate an odd series of events that had occurred at a garden centre occupying two rough sheds in Bromley, Kent. Planks of wood often mysteriously vanished, only to reappear out of the blue. A clock was seen to jump off a desk, apparently of its own accord. Then, to crown it all, garden fertilizer started falling from the ceiling, even though not stored at a height. On one occasion, it even formed the shape of a face, modelled in two distinct types of fertilizer (grey and white), on a counter. Stranger still, the skull-like shape remained static when looked at, but would disintegrate somewhat whenever Cassirer looked away. Finally, after Cassirer had investigated on two occasions, it disappeared just as mysteriously as it had arrived.

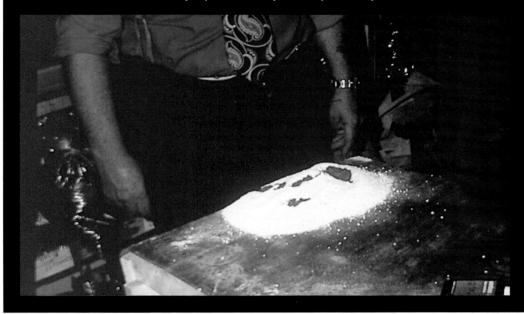

As shown in the sequence of photographs below, 12 year-old Janet seemed to be the focus of the dramatic and long-lasting Enfield poltergeist, and was often dragged out of bed by an invisible force. Even when she took to sleeping on the floor, she was still forcibly moved; and researcher Maurice Grosse, far right, always found it very difficult to hold her down.

'The 16th type are spectres which in certain times and places or homes
are wont to occasion various commotions and annoyances. I shall pass
over examples since the thing is exceedingly well known... Some disturb
slumbers with clattering of pots and hurling of stones and others pull away
a mattress and turn one out of bed.'

Although there are some people today who maintain that poltergeist activity can be attributed to 'elementals', it is more generally accepted by authorities on the subject that 'hauntings' of this kind have a natural and not a supernatural origin. Yet we still do not understand the nature of the strange forces that seem to cause them.

AN INEXPLICABLE HAUNTING

The most spectacular case ever recorded lasted from August 1977 to September 1978. During this time, a woman and her four children, who were living in a council house in Enfield, on the northern outskirts of London, experienced practically every type of poltergeist phenomenon ever identified. No fewer than 1,500 separate incidents were recorded in all, and this astonishing barrage of disturbances

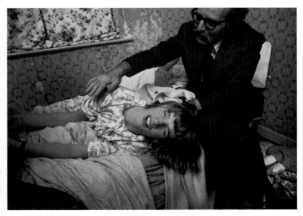

thoroughly mystified all those involved in the investigations, including social workers, a speech therapist, photographers, psychologists, priests and two poltergeist researchers.

As is usual in such cases, the 'haunting' started in a comparatively quiet fashion. A 'sort of shuffling sound' seemed to come from the floor of a bedroom, rather like the noise made by someone shambling across the room in slippers, according to the mother of the family. Then the knocking started, and this continued for nearly 11 months.

MYSTERIOUS VOICE

A voice – deep, gruff and often crude – was tape-recorded on many occasions. Several attempts were made to identify it. The voice itself claimed to belong to a 72 year-old man from a nearby road. But a listener to a local radio phone-in programme had heard a recording of the voice and identified it as that of her uncle, Bill Haylock, whom she described as a 'gypsy type'. Every attempt at proving the validity of such claims failed, however – a fairly common experience in cases of this kind.

There were many other inexplicable incidents, too. On one occasion, a toy brick suddenly appeared, flew across the room and hit a photographer on the head. Paper and pieces of cloth caught fire spontaneously, and a box of matches that was lying in a drawer burst into flames which then extin-

The phantom drummer of Tidworth – a poltergeist whose activity was recorded in 1666 – is depicted above. He produced a strange scratching or drumming noise in a bedroom that was occupied by two young girls.

Maurice Grosse, far left, has studied many household objects that were burnt or broken by the Enfield poltergeist.

The boxes of matches, left, were first set alight and then mysteriously extinguished by a London poltergeist.

guished themselves without igniting anything else in the drawer. A message, patched together from lengths of sticky tape, was also found on the lavatory door. Cutlery, a metal teapot lid and a brass pipe were all seen to bend and twist of their own accord. Three pieces of stone, found scattered about the house, were later discovered to be fragments of a single stone that had been split.

The strength of the force at work in the house can be gauged from more impressive incidents. Part of a gas fire was wrenched away from the fireplace, and its grille was thrown across the sitting-room, for instance. Large pieces of furniture, among them a chest-of-drawers, a heavy sofa and a double bed, were also tossed around the house.

Janet, the 12 year-old daughter of the house, seems to have been the epicentre or focus of all this activity, and it was from her that the mysterious deep voice seemed to emanate. She even experienced levitation (witnesses on two occasions said that she seemed to be suspended in mid-air).

She and her sister, Rose, were also thrown out of bed so often that in the end they decided to sleep on the floor; but that did not put an end to the poltergeist's activities, for Janet was often found fast asleep on top of a radio in her bedroom.

Although the family was very frightened at first, as time wore on the children and their mother became mystified rather than alarmed. Indeed, their reaction was typical of the attitude adopted by many of those who experience RSPK, as poltergeists generally cause no physical injury. As one investigator has pointed out: 'RSPK is really a series of nuisance incidents, rather like the actions of a frustrated adolescent or a child-like personality'. Interestingly, this is not entirely true of American cases, however; and experts, such as W G Roll, have noted that many victims of poltergeist activity in the United States do suffer minor physical injury.

The Enfield case was certainly remarkable for the extent and duration of the phenomena that the family experienced. But many of its features have

been observed by countless other people in other places and in other ages.

Mysterious knockings and rappings, for example, are often the first indication of the presence of a poltergeist (although some people notice first that objects are moved from their usual place). An early classic case, which became known as that of the Drummer of Tidworth, was recorded in 1666 by the Reverend Joseph Glanvill, who lived in a house on the site of the present Zouch Manor in Wiltshire. Two girls were occupying a bedroom from which a 'strange drumming sound' seemed to emerge. The noise was traced to a point 'behind the bolster'; but sceptics argued that the girls themselves were the cause. Eventually, they were cleared of suspicion. Their hands were always outside the bedclothes and, as for the noise, the Reverend Glanvill reported that he could find 'no trick, contrivance or common cause' to explain it.

SPIRIT RAPPINGS

In America, in 1848, the celebrated Fox case appeared to confirm that such raps were indeed an early indication of incipient poltergeist activity; and it was this case that actually later prompted the founding of the Spiritualist movement. Hysterical and highly imaginative witnesses assumed that spirits were trying to communicate through another two girls who were apparently (but unconsciously) responsible for the sounds that were heard.

In 1960, a similar case was investigated in Alloa in Scotland, where a girl of 11 heard a curious 'thunking' noise, rather like a ball bouncing (or a drumming sound?), that seemed to come from the head of her bed. An unusual aspect of what later developed into an extremely fascinating case was that the girl herself was so calm about the experience that investigators were able to record the incidents in a rational and detailed manner. Like the Reverend Glanvill, 300 years earlier, the Reverend Lund – one of the investigators involved in the case – found that the violent vibrations were indeed coming from the head of the bed, and he, too, ruled out the possibility of fraud.

In a case in Battersea, south London, in the 1950s, however, the poltergeist announced its arrival by placing an unidentified key on the bed of a 14 year-old girl, Shirley Hitching. This incident

Harry Hanks, top, a psychic, is seen giving his views on the Battersea poltergeist to an interviewer following a seance.

Shirley Hitching, above, was the 14 year-old focus for the Battersea 'haunting'.

Blocks of heavy paving stones, depicted right, were hurled with great violence at a coachman's house in Paris in 1846. The missiles continued to smash the house even when it was guarded by police and soldiers. Then, after several weeks, the poltergeist abruptly ceased its activities.

remained as puzzling as Shirley's ability to produce raps, several paces from her body, as a form of coded answer to questions that were put to her.

To prevent hysteria and mental stress, she and her parents, like many other victims, invented a personality for the poltergeist, whom they called Donald. They decided that he was the spirit of a 14 year-old illegitimate son of Charles II of France. Donald was irrepressible. He decorated the walls and ceiling of Shirley's bedroom with graffiti and pictures of film stars, and he wrote letters (or so it was claimed) to a number of dignitaries.

OBSCENITIES

Alien voices are a common feature of RSPK, and various theories have been advanced to explain this phenomenon. The most plausible is that put forward by a 19th-century French doctor, Gilles de la Tourette, who identified certain symptoms of severe stress, classifying them as forms of *copropraxia* (delight in the inappropriate use of obscene language) and *echolalia* (meaningless repetition of speech patterns). He further observed that some of his patients made 'obscene gestures and explosive utterances', and many of the noises and barking sounds that he described seem to have been identical to those produced by 12 year-old Janet of Enfield who, like the Frenchman's patients, was under great stress at the time (caused by, among other things, her parents' separation).

We still have to learn a very great deal about the sources of such 'commotions and annoyances', typical of poltergeist activity. But one thing is certain – the phenomenon is far too common to be ignored or explained away as the product of fevered minds. On the other hand, such experiences should probably not be taken too seriously either. Perhaps just the right blend of scepticism and acceptance was displayed by an insurance company in 1942, when it paid out £400 against an £800 claim for damage that seemed to have been caused by a poltergeist.

THE CURSE ON KILLAKEE

IT IS SAID THAT KILLAKEE HOUSE, IN DUBLIN, EIRE, ONCE STAINED BY VIOLENCE AND BLOODSHED, SUBSEQUENTLY BECAME HAUNTED AND SUBJECT TO TERRIFYING POLTERGEIST ACTIVITY. HERE, WE TAKE A LOOK AT RECENT MANIFESTATIONS OF THE HUGE CAT THAT STALKED THE HALLS OF KILLAKEE, AND AT THE DAMAGE DONE TO FURNISHINGS BY A VIOLENT, UNSEEN FORCE

A story by Edward Bulwer-Lytton, below, suggests that hauntings can be caused by their 'victims'. Did something like this happen at Killakee House?

The Victorian writer E. Bulwer-Lytton used the phrase *Haunters and Haunted* as a title for a celebrated story. He implied by the phrase that there was a definite relationship between the phenomena witnessed at a haunted house and the people who witnessed them – and that it was not a matter of chance that one person should see a ghost while another did not do so.

This certainly seems to be true in many well-attested poltergeist cases. These disturbances frequently centre on adolescents; and several researchers go so far as to claim that, in such cases, the 'haunters' emanate from the minds of the 'haunted' and are simply physical manifestations of teenage traumas. In other cases, the person most closely involved in the phenomena appears to act as a catalyst for an already well-established haunting, fanning its embers into flame by his mere presence.

A combination of these factors may have been present when Killakee House in County Dublin, Eire, became the centre of a veritable storm of psychic activity in the late 1960s and early 1970s. The onset of the phenomena occurred when new residents moved in, and ended when they left.

Killakee lies in the foothills of the Wicklow Mountains, overlooking the city of Dublin. Killakee House, built in the early 18th century as the dower house of the Massey family, is a robust, stone building with a small tower. Behind the house rises the steep slope of Montpellier Hill, its scrubby grass worn bare by the feet of those tourists hardy enough to make the ascent to the top. On the summit stands the stone shell of a fire-ravaged hunting lodge, constructed by the Earl of Rosse in the 18th century. It was used by him, and such 'bucks' as Harry Barry, first Lord Santry and Richard 'Burnchapel' Whaley, as the headquarters of the Dublin Hell Fire Club – a close imitation of the contemporary English version founded by Sir Francis Dashwood.

Rosse had a cruel sense of humour and a hatred of black cats. He used to hold court at the Eagle Tavern on Cork Hill in Dublin. On one occasion, to frighten the locals, he doused a black cat in spirits, set it alight and watched it run screaming down the hill. Dubliners swore that it was the Devil himself.

There is strong evidence that Rosse's brutal and puerile humour was also given play at the hunting lodge on Montpellier Hill. On one occasion, after a black mass, he put a black cat in the seat of honour when Satan failed to turn up in person. It was also said that a half-witted dwarf, with a twisted body and unnaturally large head, was beaten to death by Rosse and his cronies, shortly before the lodge burned down in the 1750s.

Rosse's friends often stayed with him in Killakee House, and violent scenes frequently took place there. The Irish rakes were addicted to pistol duelling. (One of the first questions asked by a prospective father-in-law of a noble suitor was 'do you blaze?', meaning 'do you fight duels?'). At least

Tom McAssey's painting, **left, is** *of the Black Cat of Killakee, which* **scared him and two companions** *one night in 1968.*

The long, low bulk of Killakee House lies beneath the hill on which the burnt-out ruin of the Hell Fire Club stands, as shown in the sketch below. *A prehistoric cairn and a standing stone existed on the hill's summit before these buildings were put up.*

three deaths from duelling took place in the grounds.

After a long interval that was relatively untroubled, there was again bloodshed at the house in the early 20th century. The house was then occupied by Countess Constance Markievicz, the 'Red Countess'. A friend of the mystical poet William Butler Yeats, she was the first woman to be elected to the House of Commons, although she never took her seat. The Countess participated in the 1916 rebellion, and five IRA men died in a gun battle at the house during her tenancy. All in all, Killakee House and the surrounding area were imbued with more violence and savagery than most reputedly haunted places.

GHOSTLY CAT

Killakee House lay empty and derelict for some years after the Second World War. Then, in the late 1960s, it was bought by Mrs Margaret O'Brien, who wanted a centre in which Irish artists and sculptors could work and exhibit. When she moved into the place in 1968, she heard stories from locals that its grounds were haunted by a black cat that was the size of an Airedale dog. 'Haunted' was an appropriate term because the stories about the cat covered a period of over 50 years – much longer than the life-span of a normal cat.

Mrs O'Brien knew some of the tales related about her new property and its environs, and was herself rather shaken when she caught glimpses of a 'big black animal' disappearing into the thick shrubbery of her garden. She thought no more

about it, however, until her friend Tom McAssey, a Dublin artist, and two colleagues had a terrifying experience one night while redecorating Killakee House in March 1968. They were working on the stone-flagged front hall, which opened on to what had been a ballroom. McAssey told a radio reporter:

'I had just locked the heavy front door, pushing a 6-inch [15-centimetre] bolt into its socket. Suddenly, one of the two men with me said that the door had opened again. We turned, startled. The lock was good and the bolt was strong, and both fastened on the inside.

'We peered into the shadowed hallway, and then I walked forward, and, sure enough, the door stood wide open, letting in a cold breeze. Outside in the darkness, I could just discern a black-draped figure, but could not see its face. I thought someone was playing a trick and said: "Come in. I see you." A low, guttural voice answered: "You can't see me. Leave this door open."

'The men standing behind me both heard the voice, but thought it spoke in a foreign language. They ran. A long, drawn-out snore came from the shadow, and in panic I slammed the heavy door and ran, too. Halfway across the gallery, I turned and looked back. The door was again open and a monstrous black cat crouched in the hall, its red-flecked, amber eyes fixed on me.'

Beside Killakee House, in a trailer in the wooded grounds, lived Val McGann, a former Irish pole-vault champion who painted and showed his work at the gallery. He showed no surprise at McAssey's story, because he had seen the huge cat on several occasions, lurking in the scraggling undergrowth.

'The first time I saw it, it frightened me stiff,' he said, 'but on subsequent occasions, I have been more interested and amazed at the size of the beast. It is about the size of a biggish dog, with terrible eyes. I've even stalked it with my shotgun, but have never been able to corner it.'

For some months after Tom McAssey's vision, apparitions were seen by workmen and artists at Killakee. They usually appeared at night, although two men reported seeing what they thought was a nun, with her back to them, at midday in the old ballroom. When they approached her, she disappeared, and a subsequent search of the house and garden failed to turn up any evidence of a real figure of any kind.

Following reports in the Dublin press and on television of the strange hauntings, a group of Irish show-business personalities persuaded Mrs O'Brien to let them try a seance in Killakee House. They included a stage conjurer who was an expert on illusions and who believed that he could rule out any 'fakery' on the part of residents. The group arranged cards carrying the letters of the alphabet in a circle on a table and placed an upturned glass in the centre. Each participant rested one finger lightly on the glass. Those who have tried this well-known technique will know that the glass will slide around the table, from letter to letter, apparently spontaneously, with no one present applying any pressure to it – consciously, at any rate. The group at Killakee asked any 'spirits' present to manifest themselves – but the 'replies' were gibberish. However, on two occasions, the lights failed, although a subsequent check of the fuses revealed no fault, and the light bulbs and wiring appeared to be completely normal. Then, two days later, events began to take a more frightening turn. First, there were bumps and knockings in the night. Lights were also switched rapidly on and off.

BELLS IN THE NIGHT

Throughout the whole of one night, the sound of door bells, in the front and back halls, could be heard. Yet those particular bells had been removed many years before.

A minor but curious manifestation was the fact that none of the residents – five or six in all – was able to sleep even on 'calm' nights. After retiring to bed exhausted from a heavy day's work, they reported lying awake, tossing and turning, and managing to sleep only after sunrise.

About four days after the seance had taken place, everyone in the house heard heavy crashes and went to investigate. To their astonishment, they found large pieces of furniture – some stored in locked rooms – thrown 'like matchboxes', some upside down, some pushed into corners. One oak medieval chair had been carefully pulled apart, joint from joint; even the brass tacks holding its tapestry in place had been pulled out and then placed in neat rows. Another similar chair had been smashed into tiny pieces.

After this outbreak, peace descended again for a matter of weeks. Then the 'haunters' turned their attention to exhibits on show in the house: a potter's works were hurled all over the room and badly smashed, while oil paintings were torn into long, narrow strips.

At this point, Margaret O'Brien sought the assistance of a priest. After obtaining permission from his superiors, he performed a Roman Catholic rite of exorcism on Killakee House. The violent outbreaks stopped, but even more bizarre incidents began to occur in their place.

Countess Markievicz, left, occupied Killakee House for a period. She was sentenced to death for her part in the 1916 uprising, but this was commuted to penal servitude for life. She was released in 1917, however, and became a noted Irish politician.

The sketch below shows the building used by the Hell Fire Club, as it was at the height of the society's infamy. It was built in about 1725 as a hunting lodge, and commanded magnificent views over the mountains and forests of the surrounding countryside. It was burned down in mysterious circumstances during one of the club's orgies of violence.

Duelling, once a legal activity, claimed the lives of several noblemen at Killakee House during the 18th century. A duel, as illustrated above, could be substituted for a trial: the defendant had the right to challenge his accuser. Even after the abolition of such judicial duels, personal combat – regulated by strict rules – remained legal between military men until it was finally outlawed in the mid-19th century.

Mrs O'Brien had still not completed furnishing her house, and she lacked a refrigerator. She had therefore asked the milkman to leave the milk in a pool in a cool stream that ran through the grounds. After the exorcism, Mrs O'Brien found that all the tinfoil tops had been removed from the bottles, although the milk was undisturbed.

Furthermore, no trace at all of the foil could be found. Mrs O'Brien assumed that it must have been carried off by birds, possibly magpies or jackdaws, attracted by its shine. To stop the nuisance, she had a heavy, four-sided box of stone built in the stream, with a large slate lid. Nevertheless, the caps continued to disappear.

THE HUMOUR OF THE HAUNTERS

At this juncture, the 'haunters' showed a trace of humour, as well as causing a rare psychic manifestation called an 'apport' – the sudden appearance of objects through apparently preternatural means. Following the disappearance of the caps from the bottles, 'caps' began to appear in the house itself, but these caps were types of headgear.

After the manifestations, Mrs O'Brien began to make a practice of locking and checking all the doors before retiring. Despite this, a profusion of small caps continued to appear all over the house. They would appear in odd places – on picture hooks or behind doors, for instance. Sometimes, rosary beads would be found, equally inexplicably.

At the end of 1970, the caps ceased to appear, although spasmodic knockings in the night continued to be heard in the house. Then, a few months later, came a discovery that might have had a grim bearing on the whole strange series of incidents. While structural alterations to the kitchen were being made, an excavation for new plumbing was

carried out. In a shallow grave a few feet under the surface, the builders found the skeleton of a dwarf, with a skull too large for its small frame – a sinister echo of the legend told of the torture carried out by the Earl of Ross and his chronies. In the grave, too, was a brass figurine, depicting a horned and tailed devil, thumbing its nose.

Once again the priest was called, this time to conduct a proper burial service on the unknown unfortunate, and after that the manifestations seemed to cease. Mrs O'Brien sold the premises six years later.

So was the Black Cat of Killakee – later portrayed in oils by artist Tom McAssey, as he had seen it on that frightening night – a manifestation that was attached to the house, or had it somehow been conjured into existence by the new occupants? Were the voices, the incessant, mysterious bells and the broken furniture results of the seance, which somehow provided a focus for them? Or was the whole series of hauntings perhaps provoked by the unhappy ghost of the dwarf, who had been brutally murdered, according to legend, by the drunken bucks of the Hell Fire Club?

It is unlikely that the answer to these questions will ever be known for sure; but we do know that all psychical phenomena ceased at the house when Joseph Frei took over the property and then added a restaurant to the art centre's facilities.

'Perhaps the previous owners were, shall we say, unlucky with the place,' he said, presumably relieved that the manifestations had ceased. 'I and my family have been very happy here – I know about the history of it, but we have only experienced a feeling of warmth and comfort. Perhaps the "haunters" like what we are doing with their "haunt".'

IT WAS AN ELDERLY 'WITCH' AND HER SECRET USE OF THE MAGICAL PENTAGRAM THAT FIRST INTRODUCED PSYCHICAL RESEARCHER TOM LETHBRIDGE TO THE WORLD OF THE PARANORMAL

Tom and Mina Lethbridge, below, were keen and accomplished dowsers.

It was at Ladram Bay, Devon, below, that Lethbridge first experienced the 'blanket of fear'.

No one who is interested in the paranormal can afford to ignore Tom Lethbridge. When he died in a nursing home in 1971, his name was hardly known to the general public. But today, many of his admirers believe that he is the single most important name in the history of psychical research. Indeed, his ideas on such subjects as dowsing, life after death, ghosts, poltergeists, magic, second-sight, precognition and the nature of time cover a wider field than those of any other psychical researcher. Moreover, they fit together into the most exciting and comprehensive theory of the 'occult' so far advanced.

These ideas were expressed in a series of small books published towards the end of his life. The odd thing is that Lethbridge took no interest in psychic matters until he retired to Devon, in southern Britain, in his mid-fifties. He had originally trained as an archaeologist and a historian, and spent most of his adult life in Cambridge as the Keeper of Anglo-Saxon Antiquities at the University Museum. But, even in that respectable setting, he was a maverick; and in 1957, he left Cambridge in disgust at the hostile reception given to one of his books on archaeology. Together with his wife, Mina, he then moved into Hole House, a Tudor mansion on the south coast of Devon. He meant to spend his retirement reading and digging for bits of broken pottery. But, in fact, the most amazing period of his eventful life was about to begin.

The person most responsible for this change of direction was an old 'witch' who lived next door. This white-haired little old lady had assured Lethbridge that she could put mild spells on people who annoyed her, and that she was able to leave her body at night and wander around the district – an ability known as 'astral projection'. Lethbridge was naturally sceptical – until something happened that finally convinced him.

The witch explained to him one day how she managed to put off unwanted visitors. What she did was to draw a five pointed star (known as a

POWER OF THE PENTAGRAM

pentagram) in her head, and then visualise it across the path of the unwanted visitor – for example, on the front gate.

Shortly afterwards, in the middle of the night, Lethbridge was lying in bed, idly drawing pentagrams in his head, and imagining them around his wife's bed, and his own, when Mina woke up with a creepy feeling that there was someone else in the room. At the foot of the bed, she could see a faint glow of light, which slowly faded as she watched it. The next day, the witch came to see them. When she told them that she had 'visited' their bedroom on the previous night, and found the beds surrounded by triangles of fire, Tom's scepticism began to evaporate; and Mina politely requested the old witch to stay out of their bedroom at night.

Three years later, the old lady died in peculiar circumstances. She had been quarrelling with a neighbouring farmer, and told Lethbridge that she intended to put a spell on the man's cattle. By this time, Lethbridge knew enough about the 'occult' to take her seriously. He warned her about the dangers of black magic, and that it could rebound on her. But the old lady ignored his advice. One morning, she was found dead in her bed – in circumstances that made the police suspect murder. The cattle of two nearby farms also suddenly developed foot and mouth disease. However, the farmer she had wanted to 'ill wish' remained unaffected. Lethbridge was convinced that the spell had gone wrong, and that it had somehow 'bounced back'.

THE INVISIBLE WORLD

The old lady's death also resulted – indirectly – in one of Lethbridge's most important insights. Passing the witch's cottage one day, he experienced a 'nasty feeling', a suffocating sense of depression. With a scientist's curiosity, he walked around the cottage, and noticed an interesting thing. He found he could step right into the depression and then out of it again, just as if it was some kind of invisible wall.

The depression reminded Lethbridge of something that had happened when he was a teenager. He and his mother had gone for a walk in the Great Wood near Wokingham. It was a lovely morning; yet, quite suddenly, both of them experienced 'a horrible feeling of gloom and depression, which crept upon us like a blanket of fog over the surface of the sea'. They hurried away, agreeing that it was something terrible and inexplicable. A few days later, the corpse of a suicide was found, hidden by some bushes, a few yards from the spot where they had been standing.

About a year after the death of the witch, another strange experience gave Lethbridge the clue he was looking for. On a damp January afternoon, he and Mina drove down to Ladram Bay. As Lethbridge stepped on to the beach, he once again experienced that feeling of gloom and fear, descending like a blanket of fog upon him. Mina wandered off along the beach, while Tom filled the sacks with seaweed. Suddenly, Mina came hurrying back, saying: 'Let's go! I can't stand this place a minute longer. There's something frightful here!'

The next day, they mentioned what had happened to Mina's brother. He said he also had experienced the same kind of thing in a field near

Hole Mill, above, was the home of Lethbridge's neighbour, a 'witch' or 'wise woman', whose strange powers convinced Lethbridge that the world of the paranormal was worth investigating. Hole House, a Tudor mansion next door, became the Lethbridges' home after Tom left Cambridge in disgust at the reception of one of his books.

Simply by visualising a pentagram, such as the one below, Lethbridge's neighbour believed she could ward off unwelcome visitors.

Avebury, in Wiltshire. Mention of the word 'field' made something connect in Tom's brain. He remembered that field telephones often short-circuit in warm, muggy weather. 'What was the weather like?' he asked. 'Warm and damp,' said his brother-in-law.

Suddenly, an idea began to take shape. Water... could that be the key? It had been warm and damp in the Great Wood, and it had been warm and damp on Ladram beach.

The following weekend, they set out for Ladram Bay a second time. Again, as they stepped on to the beach, both walked into the same bank of depression – or 'ghoul', as Lethbridge called it. Mina led Tom to the far end of the beach, to the place where she had been sitting when overwhelmed by the strange feeling. It was now so strong that it made them both feel giddy. Lethbridge described it as the feeling you get when you have a high temperature and are full of drugs. On either side of them were two small streams.

Mina wandered off to look at the scenery from the top of the cliff. Suddenly, she walked into the depression again. Moreover, she had an odd feeling, as if someone – or something – was urging her to jump over. She went to fetch Tom, who agreed that the spot was just as sinister as the place down on the seashore below.

BALEFUL SHADOW

Nine years after Lethbridge's initial experience of depression on those cliffs, a man committed suicide there. Lethbridge now wondered whether the 'ghoul' was a feeling so intense that it had become timeless, imprinting itself on the area and casting its baleful shadow on anyone who stood there. Whether from the past or from the future, feelings of despair seemed to have been 'recorded' on the surroundings – but how?

The key, Lethbridge was now convinced, lay in water. As an archaeologist, he had always been mildly interested in dowsing and water-divining. The dowser walks along with a forked hazel twig held in his hands; and when he stands above running water, the muscles in his hands and arms convulse and the twig bends either up or down. As for the mechanism involved, Professor Y. Rocard of the Sorbonne, Paris, discovered that underground water produces changes in the earth's magnetic field, and that this is what the dowser's muscles respond to.

Significantly, magnetic fields are the means by which sound is recorded on tape covered with iron oxide. Suppose the magnetic field of running water can also record strong emotions – which, after all, are basically electrical activities in the human brain and body. Such fields could well be strongest in damp and muggy weather.

MAGNETIC EMOTIONS

This would also explain why the banks of depression experienced by Lethbridge seemed to form a kind of invisible wall. Anyone who has ever tried bringing a magnet closer and closer to an iron nail will know that the nail is suddenly 'seized' by the magnet as it enters the force field. Presumably, the magnetic field of water has the same property. And if it can 'tape record' powerful emotions, then you would feel them quite suddenly, as you stepped into the field. Both Tom and Mina had noticed that the 'ghoul' they experienced on Ladram beach came to an end quite abruptly

Lethbridge was also convinced that his electrical theory applied to ghosts. In 1922, when an undergraduate at Cambridge, he had seen a ghost in the rooms of a friend. He had been just about to leave, late at night, when the door opened and a man wearing a top hat came in. Assuming he was a college porter who had come to give his friend a message, Lethbridge said goodnight, and went out. The man did not reply.

The next morning, Lethbridge saw his friend, and asked casually about the identity of the man in the top hat. His friend flatly denied that anyone had come in. When Lethbridge brooded on it, he realised that the man had not in fact worn a porter's uniform, but hunting kit. So why had he not recognised the red coat at the time? Lethbridge then recalled that it had been grey – a dull grey, like a monochrome photograph. So it was that Lethbridge realised he had seen a ghost. Moreover, his friend's rooms overlooked the river, so there was a damp atmosphere.

Tom had also seen a ghost in the witch's garden, the year before she died. He had been sitting on the hillside, looking down at the witch's house, when he suddenly noticed two women who were

> ❝ ALTHOUGH HE [LETHBRIDGE]
> WAS INCLINED TO BELIEVE THAT
> GHOSTS ARE TAPE RECORDINGS,
> HE ALSO BELIEVED THAT THERE
> IS A REALM BEYOND DEATH THAT IS,
> TO SOME EXTENT, ACCESSIBLE TO
> LIVING CREATURES. ❞
>
> **COLIN WILSON, MYSTERIES**

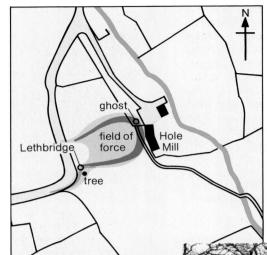

metres 0 ____ 50
feet 0 50 100 150

Lethbridge saw the ghost of an old lady and experienced a curious tingling sensation when he stood over an underground stream, at the spot shown right. He later discovered that the two experiences were connected.

The map, left, shows the position of the ghost seen at Hole Mill in relation to the underground stream and its field of force. Lethbridge plotted the area 'blind' with his hazel twig. Later excavation showed him to be correct in every detail.

The Reverend Bishop Leonidas Polk, below, intrigued Professor Joseph Buchanan in the 1840s by being able to detect brass in the dark, simply by touching it with his fingers.

in the yard. One was the witch; the other was a tall old lady dressed in rather old-fashioned grey clothes. Later, he saw the witch and asked her about her visitor. The witch looked puzzled. Then, when Lethbridge described the figure, she said: 'Ah, you've seen my ghost.'

This happened in 1959, before Lethbridge had his important insight on Ladram beach. So it never even entered his head that the ghost was a form of 'tape recording'. His first thought was that the old lady in grey might be some kind of thought-projection – in other words, a kind of 'television picture', caused by someone else thinking about the ghost, and somehow transferring the thought into his own mind. Then it struck him that ghosts are supposed to reappear on anniversaries. So he and Mina decided that they would go to the same spot, at the same time, the following year, to see if anything would happen.

They stood quietly at the same spot, on a fine, warm morning, but the old lady failed to reappear.

However, Lethbridge and his wife sensed a kind of electrical tingling in the atmosphere. There was a tiny underground stream running down the lane – under a drain cover – and they felt the tingling most strongly when standing on top of it. Lethbridge was only to realise the significance of that tingling feeling after his experience on Ladram beach. He then decided to explore the stream and see where it led. The result confirmed his suspicions. The stream turned at right angles quite close to the witch's house; and it was directly above this stream that he had seen the ghost of the old lady in grey. He had been connected to the spot, it seemed, by the magnetic field of the flowing water. But the witch, standing a few yards away from the underground stream, had seen nothing.

So Lethbridge had been quite mistaken to believe that his 'old lady' was some kind of 'television picture' projected by someone else's mind, or a ghost that would return exactly a year later. It was almost certainly just another 'recording', but in black and white, just like the huntsman he had seen in his friend's rooms at Cambridge.

It would be very satisfying to be able to add that Lethbridge decided to investigate the apparitions, and found that a huntsman had died of apoplexy in the room in Cambridge, or that the old lady had drowned in the underground stream. But no such neat, satisfactory solutions can be provided – and neither are they necessary. The huntsman had probably been a previous inhabitant of the rooms; and the old lady had probably lived most of her life in Hole Mill – the witch's house. (From her clothes, Lethbridge thought she dated back to before the First World War.) But there is no earthly reason why the 'force field' of water should record only unpleasant emotions. The old lady might have been unusually happy or excited when she was 'photographed'. Or perhaps she passed over the spot so often that her image finally became indelibly imprinted there.

How much evidence is there for the Lethbridge theory of ghosts? To begin with, it is worth noting that his 'tape recording' theory was by no means new. In America, in the 1840s, a professor named Joseph Rhodes Buchanan was intrigued when a

American professor Joseph Rhodes Buchanan believed that all substances – even a tree, such as that illustrated **above** – have a force field around them, on which human feelings can be recorded, to be 'played back' later.

In the mid-19th century, William Denton gave a piece of volcanic rock to a sensitive who immediately saw a volcano erupt, such as the one **below**. This was one of the first serious experiments into psychometry (or object-reading).

certain Bishop Polk told him that he could detect brass in the dark by touching it with his fingers, since it produced an unpleasant taste in his mouth. Buchanan tested him and found it was true. He discovered that certain of his students also had the same curious ability. In fact, some of them could even detect different substances when these were wrapped up in brown paper. Buchanan decided that the nerves produce some kind of force field – he called it the 'nerve aura' – which streams out of the finger ends, and which operates like an extra sense.

A STRANGE TALENT

What really puzzled him was that some of his sensitives could hold a sealed letter and describe the person who had written it, remarking upon whether the writer was sad or happy at the time. Buchanan explained this by suggesting that all substances give off emanations (or force fields) on which human emotions can be recorded.

Buchanan's friend, William Denton, a professor of geology, took the theory even further. He tried wrapping a piece of Hawaiian volcanic rock in paper and handing it to a sensitive, who immediately saw in his mind an island in the midst of blue seas, and an exploding volcano. When handed a pebble of glacial limestone, the sensitive saw it frozen in deep ice; and the fragment of a meteor produced a picture of the depths of space, with glittering stars. Denton was so excited by all this that he believed he had discovered a new – or forgotten – human faculty, and that one day we shall be able to look back into the past just as easily as we can now look at stars (which may have died millions of years ago) through a telescope.

Buchanan and Denton called this strange faculty *psychometry*, and for a few years it caused considerable excitement in the scientific world. Then, with the influence of Darwin, a more sceptical climate began to prevail, and it was forgotten. Even so, Sir Oliver Lodge, the notable scientist who dared to be interested in psychical research, wrote in 1908:

'Take, for example, a haunted house. . . wherein some one room is the scene of a ghostly representation of some long past tragedy. On a psychometric hypothesis, the original tragedy has been literally photographed on its material surroundings, nay, even on the ether itself, by reason of the intensity of emotion felt by those who enacted it.'

It may seem that Lethbridge's discovery was not so remarkable after all: but to believe this would be a mistake, for it was to prove only part of a far more comprehensive and important general theory of the paranormal.

" I MUST STICK TO MY ORIGINAL THESIS THAT THE SUPERNATURAL WILL CONFORM TO NATURAL LAWS, EVEN IF WE DO NOT KNOW THE LAWS AS YET. **"**

T.C. LETHBRIDGE,

GHOST AND GHOUL

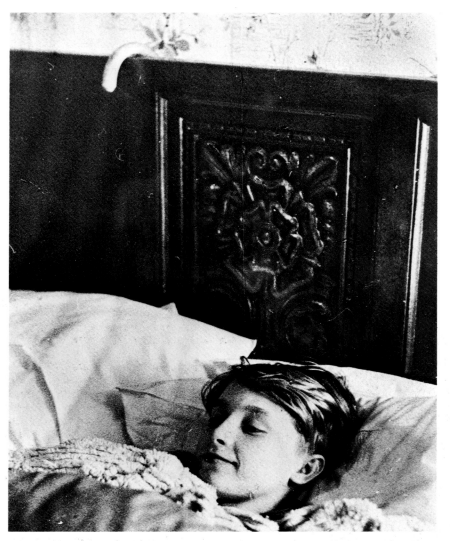

IT HAS LONG BEEN HELD THAT AT THE CENTRE OF ANY POLTERGEIST ACTIVITY WILL BE FOUND A DISTURBED ADOLESCENT GIRL. BUT EXPERTS NOW BELIEVE THAT SEXUAL TENSION IN YOUNG OR OLD, MALE OR FEMALE, MAY CAUSE THE PHENOMENON

As more and more cases of poltergeist activity are subjected to rigorous investigation by parapsychologists, a clearer picture is emerging not only of the possible causes of such phenomena, but also of those who are generally the victims. There are, of course, cases that evade classification, but research into recurrent spontaneous psychokinesis (RSPK) appears to support certain broad conclusions.

The sexual drive, or libido, seems to be at the root of many paranormal experiences. In the 1840s, for instance, when the case of the Fox sisters stirred up a great deal of interest in the United States and elsewhere, it was widely assumed that the girls' experiences were associated with the fact that they had just reached puberty. Other cases that were examined at that time appeared to confirm the assumption that girls on the threshold of sexual maturity were to be blamed for all such

SEX AND THE MISCHIEVOUS SPIRIT

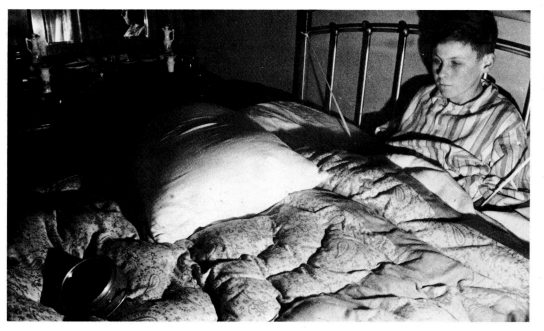

The 10-year-old boy, above, was being filmed when the walking-stick hanging from his bed head jerked and jumped about of its own accord.

12-year-old Alan Rhodes, left, had his hands taped to the bedclothes to guard against trickery when his poltergeist was investigated by researcher Harry Price in 1945. Even so, the alarm clock managed to jump on to his bed, and was later joined by a trinket case from the dressing table.

mysterious incidents: only young women, it was thought, could summon up reserves of energy capable of moving tables, producing strange sounds and causing objects to appear and disappear – the familiar signs of poltergeist activity.

Certainly, many cases today also involve girls at about the age of puberty. In the classic case of the family living in the London suburb of Enfield, who experienced intense and protracted disturbances between 1977 and 1978, for example, Janet – the 12-year-old daughter – was clearly the epicentre. Shirley Hitchings of Battersea, another famous victim of poltergeist activity, was 14 years old at the time. One middle-aged mother with a 12-year-old daughter, meanwhile, told a parapsychologist that her family had experienced a number of incidents of RSPK during the course of a few weeks, both in the kitchen and in her daughter's bedroom.

'Bumps, crashes and saucepans flying about – you know, the usual type of thing. But when Sheila started her menses, it all stopped, of course. It was all a bit of a nuisance at the time, but we are all right now.'

Eleanora Zugun, above, would develop mysterious marks on her face whenever she felt insulted.

Rappings regularly disturbed the Fox family, above, in a case that helped to establish the assumption that poltergeist activity was particularly associated with young girls.

Apart from the onset of puberty, another common feature has been observed in young victims of RSPK. Janet and her sister in Enfield were obsessed with Starsky and Hutch, the heroes of a television series; Shirley Hitchings adored James Dean, the film star; and another poltergeist victim was infatuated with Dr Who, the character in a major science fiction serial. It has been suggested that this sort of passion, involving fictional characters, serves to ensure that the powerful force deployed by such girls is unconstrained by the influences of normal day-to-day life.

Such isolation from the norm was even more apparent in the case of a young Romanian peasant girl, Eleanora Zugun, who was able, between the ages of 12 and 15, to produce marks on her body whenever she felt that her personal 'devil' was being insulted. At the slightest word or gesture that she interpreted as offensive, scratches and bites would appear on her face and arms.

Although young girls are often the focus of RSPK, however, it has been observed that they are rarely the sole agents of the disturbances. In the

" AT FIVE MINUTES PAST MIDNIGHT ON MONDAY, 16 DECEMBER 1968, I WAS WALKING BEHIND TWELVE-YEAR-OLD ROGER CULLIHAN AS HE ENTERED THE KITCHEN OF HIS HOUSE. WHEN HE CAME TO THE SINK, HE TURNED TOWARD ME AND AT THAT MOMENT THE KITCHEN TABLE... JUMPED INTO THE AIR, ROTATED ABOUT 45 DEGREES AND CAME TO REST ON THE BACKS OF THE CHAIRS THAT STOOD AROUND IT... **"**

DR W.G. ROLL, THE POLTERGEIST

Fox case, for instance, two sisters out of three were involved; and at Enfield, both Janet and her sister were at the centre of many of the incidents. (Interestingly, another family member, Janet's brother, was at the time attending a school for the mentally subnormal; subnormality is often – though by no means always – associated with outbreaks of poltergeist activity.)

In some cases, girls are not involved at all, though a hundred years ago, male victims of RSPK were often ignored or discounted, so entrenched was the view that pubescent girls were always the source of poltergeist activity. The experiences of one sensitive, D.D. Home, did provoke more serious examination of paranormal incidents associated with men, however; but investigators were content to conclude that Home was a homosexual and left the matter there.

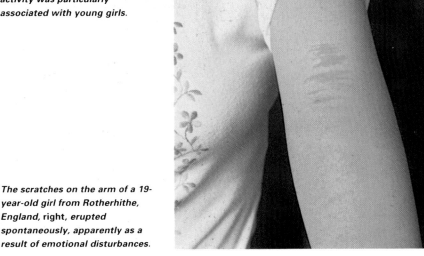

In recent years, male sensitives, young boys and men alike, have received a more sympathetic hearing. One 10-year-old boy was filmed as he lay in bed, awake, while a walking-stick moved of its own accord, in erratic jerks, behind the head of his bed. Like many young epicentres, he was of an extremely nervous disposition and, again in common with other victims, was anaemic.

Another fascinating case involved two boys in Glasgow, between August 1974 and May 1975. The boys were 15 and 11 years old, and lived with their parents in a tenement flat. A series of 'peculiar sounds' was heard, followed by communicative raps. It turned out that the boys, without knowing it, were linked telepathically with an old man who lived in a flat on the ground floor and who was afflicted by a malignant tumour. As the old man's condition deteriorated, the raps became more frequent. They ceased, suddenly, when the old man died. But perhaps the most celebrated case of all is that of Matthew Manning – the well-known healer – who, at the age of 11, was able to produce a variety of genuine phenomena at will. Disturbances occurred both at his Cambridge home and at school: beds moved; stones appeared inexplicably; and sudden cold spots were discovered. His brother and sister, meanwhile, seemed to be unaffected by the experiences.

But it would be inaccurate to assume that RSPK is linked exclusively with puberty. Indeed, a survey carried out in the 1950s indicated that seven was the age at which most children were particularly sensitive and receptive, and this finding has been confirmed by subsequent studies – although children as young as four or five have also been identified as epicentres. Most are quite unaware that they are responsible for the disturbances. Their powers vary: some, like Shirley Hitchings, have to 'screw up their eyes as if concentrating' in order to produce intelligent raps; and many of the children who are able to bend metal (in the manner of Uri Geller) have only to gaze at the object for a moment or two, and then glance away, for the metal to move or twist.

The Harper family from Enfield, left, were affected by some of the most elaborate and remarkable poltergeist activity on record.

At the other end of the age range, adults long past the age of puberty also experience poltergeist activity, although in many cases there does appear to be an unequivocal link between sexuality and RSPK. Interestingly, the majority of mediums who provoke – or claim to provoke – physical phenomena are women in their middle years, who have reached the menopause, when their metabolism is disturbed, much as it is at puberty. In this connection, it is worth mentioning that Janet's mother, at Enfield, was just at that age – a fact that may well have contributed to the intensity of the poltergeist activity in the household. Among mediums of both sexes, there are also those who admit to sexual frustration and who acknowledge that seances provide a form of sexual release.

PENT-UP EMOTION

Sexual maladjustment may indeed contribute to, or heighten, sensitivity; and certainly, a number of recent cases suggest that RSPK may be related to frustration and distress. One involved a man of 48, who was living with his elderly uncle in a large house in York, England. Whenever the younger man entered his study, the room appeared to react to his presence: his desk moved; chairs shuffled across the floor; the curtains blew into the room even on airless days; and the windows would open and shut rapidly. Such incidents persisted for nearly three years, increasing in frequency and intensity all the time, until mental exhaustion eventually forced the man to seek medical assistance. He was found to be sexually impotent and given treatment. Within a week, the phenomena ceased.

Another case was that of a family of four who lived in Somerset, south-west England. For some months, the household had been disrupted by paranormal incidents of all kinds, and the two teenage children were assumed to be the cause. But when the case was investigated, it appeared to be the father, and not the children, who was the source of the disturbance. He was a professional man of 49, who had become increasingly concerned about his promotion prospects at work, had developed insomnia and had become sexually impotent. Anxiety finally pushed him towards the brink of breakdown. But once he had been given the help and encouragement that he needed, the family experienced no further disruption.

A similarly strange case of this kind was documented in Bavaria, in Germany, in 1967. A number of inexplicable incidents were observed by employees at the office of a lawyer, accompanied by an alarming increase in the size of the telephone bill. The electricity and telephone companies were alerted and requested to check all equipment in the building, and Professor Hans Bender undertook an investigation of the case. A survey of the numbers dialled from the office revealed that one particular number was constantly being activated, though no one was dialling it: the number was that of the speaking clock, O119. Eventually, Professor Bender traced the incidents to the source – a 19-year-old girl called Anne-Marie. He concluded that she was dissatisfied with her working conditions and was generally unhappy, for she seemed to have a remarkable effect on the machines in the office, which she admitted she disliked, and on other electrical

Anne-Marie Schneider, below, sent her employer's telephone bill soaring when her poltergeist constantly dialled the speaking clock. Once she married, however, the activity ceased.

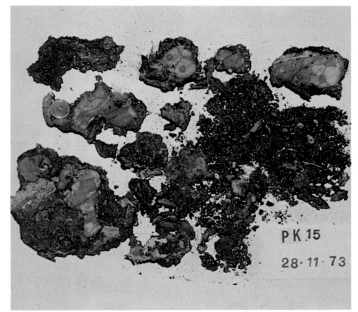

Two worrying cases of spontaneous combustion – a feature of poltergeist activity – both involved girls in Brazil. One, which affected a family in Sao Paulo for six years, caused clothes to be set on fire inside a closed wardrobe and reduced them to ashes, as shown above left; *while the other, occurring in Suzano in 1970, burned the wardrobe,* above right. *When the police were called, they too became the victims of mysterious fires.*

Council house tenants Mary Sharman and her two sons, left, *were victims of poltergeist disturbances for 12 years. The trouble stopped when the family moved house.*

But perhaps the most significant finding of recent research is that 86 per cent of all poltergeist activity is experienced by families that have recently moved into council houses. It is not hard to find an explanation for this. Any move is bound to be disturbing; and in these circumstances, it is hardly surprising that tension generated by the members of the family, both individually and as a group, should provoke incidents and noises that cannot be readily explained away, or that ultimately many families – frightened and distraught – should demand to be rehoused.

Any attempt to provide a definitive categorisation of actual and potential poltergeist epicentres needs to be based on thorough psychological and medical examination of all victims who can be identified, but such examinations are hardly ever conducted. Investigators have, on the whole, been too anxious to record incidents, or to eliminate the possibility of fraud, to concern themselves with study of the mental and physical state of victims and their families.

> ❚❚ THE POLTERGEIST WAS PLAYING UP EVERY TIME HE WENT TO SEE HIS GIRLFRIEND AND TORMENTED HER IN HIS ABSENCE. IT TORMENTED HIM, TOO, AT NIGHT. IT WOULD GET HOLD OF HIM IN BED, AND HOLD HIM FAST WHILE IT TICKLED HIS FACE AND TUGGED HIS HAIR. ❚❚
> MARY WILLIAMS,
> THE POLTERGEIST MAN, JOURNAL
> OF ANALYTICAL PSYCHOLOGY, VOL. 8

equipment. Overhead lamps would swing to and fro whenever she passed underneath them, and the fluid in photo-copying machines would spill on to the floor. The only plausible explanation for the steep rise in the telephone bill was that Anne-Marie was bored with her job and was mentally clock-watching, stimulating a response from the speaking clock. On the day that Anne-Marie was married, all such incidents seemed to cease.

Sexual maladjustment is not the only source of tension or distress, however: indeed, researchers believe that RSPK may be related to many other conditions. Migraine and temporal lobe epilepsy are common among middle-aged epicentres and sensitives, for example; and there is evidence to suggest that there could be some link between these disorders and 'psychic' faculties. It has even been observed that the parents of many young epicentres hold conflicting religious views, which appear to trigger distress in their children that in turn leads to outbreaks of RSPK.

ANIMAL EXTRAS

SPIRIT PHOTOGRAPHY, WHETHER BY AMATEURS OR PROFESSIONALS, HAS ITS GALLERY OF GHOSTLY CATS, DOGS AND OTHER ANIMALS – USUALLY PETS – THAT APPEAR AS UNEXPECTED 'EXTRAS'

The majority of spirit photographs in which animal 'extras' appear have been taken unintentionally, generally by amateurs who have been most surprised to find these curious additional images on their films, but who have usually managed to recognise the identity of the unexpected ghostly forms.

An interesting example of this is a picture taken by Major Wilmot Allistone at Clarens, in Switzerland, in August 1925. At first glance, it seems a somewhat badly composed family snap, but on closer inspection it reveals itself as a remarkable psychic photograph. The Major was surprised and intrigued to discover that the developed print bore the faint image of a white semi-transparent kitten, nestling above the right hand of his son, alongside the furry toy animal that the child held in his left hand. The boy had held no such kitten when the picture was being taken. But what astonished the

The Allistone family are seen above, together with a surprising 'extra' in the form of a kitten. It showed up as though nestled in the boy's hand, along with the toy he held, seen clearly in the detail. The most astonishing thing about the spirit animal was that it resembled the child's recently killed pet.

Major was the fact that this ghostly kitten closely resembled the boy's pet, which had died a few days previously, having been mauled by a St Bernard dog.

The negative and prints of this fascinating photograph were later submitted to extensive investigation by experts, who even studied the negative under a stereoscopic microscope. The appearance of the dead pet was never explained.

Another example, in some respects even more peculiar, is a picture that was submitted to the British College of Psychic Science in 1927. This was a simple photograph of Lady Hehir and her Irish wolfhound Tara, taken by a Mrs Filson. The picture proved to be far from ordinary, however. The extra in this case is no semi-transparent wraith but a very substantial puppy head, curiously misplaced at the rear end of the wolfhound. Both Mrs Filson and Lady Hehir recognised this disjointed 'extra' as the

Cairn puppy, Kathal, which had been a close companion of the wolfhound. It had died in August 1926, about six weeks before the picture was actually taken.

In her signed declaration submitted to the college, Lady Hehir remarked: 'I feel convinced that he [the Cairn puppy] is often in the room with Tara and me, as she talks in a soft cooing way to something she evidently sees'.

INVISIBLE FORMS

One cannot have pets for very long without observing that they appear at times to see visitants invisible to the human eye – whether these are ghosts, elementals, or some other sort of being is open to discussion. However, one unusual photograph shows a pet actually watching a form that was invisible to the photographer at the time. It was intended to be an ordinary flash picture of Monet, a pet cat, taken by his owner Alfred Hollidge in 1974. The Hollidge family had only one cat, and there was certainly no other cat in the house when the picture was being taken. But the developed negatives showed a dark animal running in front of Monet – a small kitten, or a large rat, with a curiously long, tail-like attachment trailing behind. There is no way of being sure what Hollidge himself saw, for he left the negatives for some months before sending them off for processing, and he died before they were returned – so he never examined the final prints. But it is more than likely that he would have remarked on anything strange when taking the photograph, and would have been anxious to see the prints had he observed the dark intruder. Perhaps

The photograph, above, shows a pet cat and a ghostly dark intruder that was unseen by the photographer – but the cat seems to be watching it with intense concentration.

A Cairn puppy, below, dead about six weeks, makes a curiously out-of-place appearance on this picture of its mistress and the wolfhound that was its close companion in life.

the most interesting thing about this spirit photograph is that Monet does seem to be watching something in the area in which the extra appeared on the print.

But a number of spirit photographs with animal 'extras' have been taken by professionals. The well-established American psychic photographer Edward Wyllie, for instance, took a picture in which the spirits of both a woman and a dog appeared. It was taken in Los Angeles, California, in 1897 for J. Wade Cunningham, who later sent the English journalist and Spiritualist, William T. Stead, a long account of its making.

According to Cunningham, a female medium would often tell him of the beautiful woman who would sometimes appear when he was present. This spirit woman was frequently accompanied by a dog that barked and jumped with delight at the sound of Cunningham's voice. One day, the medium asked the spirit if she would be prepared to bring the dog and sit for a photograph. Wyllie, not knowing what was expected of him, was commissioned to make this spirit picture. The print he produced revealed both the beautiful woman and the dog, which Cunningham happily recognised as a pet he had owned many years before.

WISHFUL THINKING

The English medium and psychic photographer, William Hope, rarely took open-air pictures; but while on holiday in Exmouth, Devon, in 1924, he took some snapshots of his assistant, Mrs Buxton, and her family on the steps of their caravan. The print is badly faded now, but it is still possible to see a number of curious extras. Mrs Buxton herself is all but blotted out by an ectoplasmic cloud, and above her, swathed in this mist, is an image of the face of her son, who had died the previous year. She later said that, while the picture was being taken, she was 'wishing that he could have been one of the group'.

Alongside the son's head and to the right, there is also a form that clearly resembles the head of a horse or pony. In further tremendous excitement, the family recognised this as the son's white pony, called Tommy, which had died just a short time before the son. A third 'extra' is somewhat harder to see. This is superimposed over Mr Buxton's

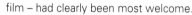

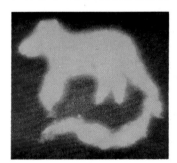

waistcoat, and is the image of an old man. Mr Buxton reported that it was a portrait of his brother, who had died some time previously.

The faded quality of this Hope picture provides a reminder that, for some mysterious reason, very few spirit photographs survive the ravages of time. It is a pity that the one made by the little-known psychic photographer Dr Stanbury in the 1880s could not be preserved.

PSYCHIC SNAPS

It seems that a certain Mrs Cabell had formerly owned two dogs – one, an old carriage dog with the fancy name of Secretary Stanton; the other, a small black-and-tan named Fanny. The two dogs were close friends, and they had died of old age within a few hours of each other. Some four years after their deaths, Mrs Cabell was spending the summer at Onset Bay in Massachusetts, USA, and was invited to a seance.

During the course of the evening, the medium observed on the psychic plane a 'little wee bit of a dog' jumping around Mrs Cabell, and when she examined the collar, she found the name 'Fanny' was inscribed upon it. Mrs Cabell was, of course, very excited, and took up with interest the suggestion that they should visit Dr Stanbury, who was nearby, to see if he could take a picture of her old pet. Mrs Cabell later told this story:

'Imagine my surprise at seeing my little pet cuddle up under my arm. And my surprise I cannot express at seeing the old coachdog, Stanton, also. He occupied the most prominent position, and had almost crowded out of sight his little friend in his eagerness to get there himself... The dogs' pictures have been recognised by hundreds of people who knew them when in life... It was four years after their death, or passing away, when this photograph was taken, which I prize beyond all price.' For Mrs Cabell, the reappearance of her pets – if only on film – had clearly been most welcome.

Other animals also appear in the seance room at times. A sort of ape creature appeared on a photograph of the famous Polish medium, Franek Kluski, who was also photographed with an owl-like bird hovering over his back. This bird, which seems almost to be attacking Kluski, was not seen in the room before or after the seance. A totally unexplained image of a bat-like creature appeared above a cloud of ectoplasm in a picture taken by Staveley Bulford, a member of the British College of Psychic Science, in 1921. The cadaverous humanoid face of the bat appears to have been built out of a special kind of ectoplasm, which Bulford himself described as 'a quite different kind of ectoplasm, very dense and quite non-luminous'.

The series of seances that produced the ectoplasmic bat were conducted in the photographic studio of a certain Mr Scott between May and July 1921. He produced some extraordinary psychic pictures, as well as later 'communications' from the photographed spirits.

Further pictures that were obtained during these experimental seances were varied in subject matter, though they also included the 'standard' portrait of spirits, swathed in ectoplasmic cotton wool or other curiously unrelated ectoplasmic structures. One, however, was of a plant. It was extremely clear and detailed, in the form of a spray with thick velvety leaves, and flowers that were reminiscent of an edelweiss. The animal world was also represented in a photograph taken of Scott himself: above his head there appeared a quaint animal with a long, winding tail, again within a cloud of shiny ectoplasm.

While many psychic photographers tried deliberately to catch human spirits with the camera, few made a conscious effort to photograph animal spirits. Perhaps this is why such animal 'extras' occur comparatively rarely.

Soon after they moved into the Bull's Head, a number of strange things started happening to Pamela Flamerty and her family. A poltergeist, it seemed, had moved in with them, too

AFTER-TIME VISITOR

When my former husband, Richard, and I took over the Bull's Head at Swinton, near Manchester, in January 1985, none of us was prepared for the strange and almost tragic events which were about to unfold.

The pub, established during the 16th century, but rebuilt in 1826, is steeped in history. Thinking about it now, it seems just the place for a poltergeist; but paranormal researchers have since told me that the pub had no long tradition 'of being haunted'. For us, it all began in February of the year we moved in.

The accounts office is safely situated in a room off the cellar. After closing time, the thick stone walls make it deathly quiet in there. One night, I was in the room alone, checking figures by the side of the only door. Suddenly, a scraping sound from behind spoiled my concentration. I turned, and was absolutely astonished to see a small stool moving across the floor of its own accord. It did this several times, moving back and forth. It seemed as if someone must have been pushing it – except, of course, no one else was there.

The next strange thing occurred one afternoon when our children were downstairs. My youngest son suddenly ran up to our flat in something of a panic. 'Mum, there's a man in the pub', he said.

I told him not to be silly: the pub was closed. But he was insistent, and I followed him to where his brother was waiting. There was no one there by now, but the boys were certain that a man wearing a blue jumper had been sitting in one of the corners. All of the doors were still locked, and no one was lurking in the toilets. A previous manager later described to us a similar apparition of a man in a blue jumper.

Another frightening episode occurred one evening when we were preparing to go to bed. The building was secure, the alarms set, and Richard and I had begun to go upstairs. The landing lights were always left on during the night, in case one of the boys wanted to visit the bathroom. Yet, as we made our way along the corridor, one by one the bulbs went out. There was no rational explanation: if a fuse had blown, all the lights would have gone out simultaneously. We were far too frightened to investigate, so we locked the bedroom door.

It was then that we heard the footsteps. They were clear, but sounded as if they were on stone, not wooden boards. Eventually we managed a few hours' sleep. In the morning, every light in the building was on, including those in the bar, which we quite clearly remembered switching off.

But a worse incident was to occur, in which my stepfather could have lost his life. On Easter Sunday, we had decided to hold a small party after closing time. Quite late on, we were gathered around the bar, chatting, when someone brought up the subject of the resident 'ghost'. Several staff had complained of 'cold spots', and some even claimed to have seen an apparition in the cellar.

At the height of the discussion, one of the guests challenged both Steve McRea, a family friend, and my stepfather, to spend the night in the cellar. They agreed. Later, when everyone else had left or gone to bed, we led them down the narrow,

> **❝** UNLOCKING THE CELLAR DOOR, WE FOUND STEVE CROUCHING IN A DEFENSIVE POSTURE, TERROR WRITTEN ALL OVER HIS FACE. **❞**

twisting stone steps, and finally into the basement.

We made sure they were comfortable, and Richard and I then went to get some sleep, after switching off the lights and securely locking the cellar door. This meant that no one could get down into the cellar; but equally, as we realised afterwards, no one could get out.

We were woken up some time later by several dreadful screams emanating from the bowels of the building. Richard and I rushed downstairs. Unlocking the cellar door, we found Steve crouching in a defensive posture, terror written all over his face. My stepfather, meanwhile, lay motionless at the foot of the steps, blood gushing from his head.

Apparently they had chatted for a while, still

The Bull's Head at Swinton, where a mysterious visitor took up residence in 1985.

treating the whole thing as a joke, before dozing off. Later in the night, my stepfather was woken by the sound of Steve shouting. There, framed by the alcove opposite, were several orange and red lights, resembling a row of vertical metre-long fluorescent tubes. Then, suddenly, there was a flash, and the lights were gone.

It was at this point that my stepfather decided to make a dash for the cellar steps. But just as he was about to move, an invisible hand suddenly gripped his left shoulder, and then a voice whispered harshly in his ear: 'Derek...'

That was the last thing he remembered until he regained consciousness. The injury had been caused by my stepfather tripping over a beer barrel as he lost his footing; but whether he had fallen or was pushed, it remains uncertain.

We moved out of the Bull's Head just before Christmas of that year, after a final episode during which 'someone' invisible had started playing tricks on our telephone line, as confirmed by an engineer. When he tried to dial the test number, he seemed to encounter difficulties.

He tried again, and asked if there was anyone using the downstairs 'phone. Richard assured him that we were the only people in the building, but I checked anyway. The 'phone was resting in its cradle and everything seemed normal. He tried again and then, in exasperation, turned to me and said: 'Someone's downstairs on the other 'phone.'

I went back down and, this time, the 'phone was off the hook. By then, we were quite used to odd things happening. I don't know whether we had triggered something off which had previously lain dormant; but I do know that, since we have left, the haunting has continued, albeit to a lesser, more benign degree.

VOICES FROM THE DEAD

HAS THE MODERN TAPE RECORDER PROVIDED EVIDENCE OF SURVIVAL AFTER DEATH? THOUSANDS OF VOICES – PURPORTING TO BE THOSE OF THE DEAD – HAVE BEEN RECORDED WITHOUT RATIONAL EXPLANATION FOR THEIR ORIGIN. WHAT ARE WE TO MAKE OF THEM?

Thomas Alva Edison was one of the greatest practical scientists of the 19th century. His achievements included the perfection of the 'duplex' telegraph, the invention of the phonograph and the introduction into the United States of the first electric light. In 1882, his generating station brought electric street lighting to New York for the first time; and 12 years later, his moving picture show, which he called his 'kinetoscope parlour', was opened in the city.

Despite such solid successes, however, an interview he gave to the *Scientific American* in 1920 caused concern among his contemporaries, some of whom must have thought that the 73-year-old inventor had lapsed into senility. What he proposed, in the issue of 30 October, was no less than an instrument for communicating with the dead.

'If our personality survives, then it is strictly logical and scientific to assume that it retains memory, intellect and other faculties and knowledge that we acquire on this earth. Therefore, if personality exists after what we call death, it is reasonable to conclude that those who leave this earth would like to communicate with those they have left here...

I am inclined to believe that our personality hereafter will be able to affect matter. If this reasoning be correct, then, if we can evolve an instrument so delicate as to be affected, or moved, or manipulated... by our personality as it survives in the next life, such an instrument, when made available, ought to record something.'

Edison worked on the development of such an instrument, but was unsuccessful in his attempts to record voices from the dead. However, in the opinion of many modern scientific researchers, his views were apparently vindicated in 1959.

GHOSTS IN THE MACHINE

At that time, a celebrated Swedish painter, musician and film producer named Friedrich Jürgenson took his battery-operated tape recorder out into a remote part of the countryside near his villa in order to record birdsong. Playing the tapes back later, Jürgenson found not only bird sounds but faint

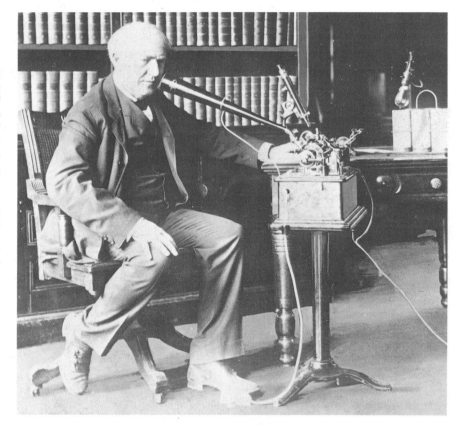

Thomas Alva Edison (1847-1931), above, invented the phonograph and the electric light bulb. In 1920 he also worked on a device that would, he believed, make possible a form of telepathic contact with the dead.

human voices, speaking in Swedish and Norwegian and discussing nocturnal birdsong. Despite the 'coincidence' of subject matter, Jürgenson first thought that he had picked up a stray radio transmission. On repeating the experiment, however, he heard further voices, this time addressing him personally and claiming to be dead relatives, as well as friends of his.

Over the next few years, working from his home at Mölnbo, near Stockholm, Jürgenson amassed the evidence that he was to present in his book *Voices from the Universe* in 1964. This proved sufficiently convincing to attract the attention of the eminent German psychologist Professor Hans Bender, director of the Government-funded parapsychological research unit at the University of Freiburg, who in turn set up a team of distinguished scientists to repeat the experiments and analyse the results.

PERSPECTIVES

RECORDING THE VOICES YOURSELF

An ordinary cassette tape recorder can be used to record 'electronic voices'; but, generally speaking, the better the equipment, the more satisfactory the results. Machines with volume, tone and level controls make the task of deciphering the voices on playback much easier, and a good set of headphones is essential.

Experts agree that the hours between sunset and sunrise are the best time for experiments. Most researchers prefer to work in a quiet room, although a portable tape recorder in a quiet place in the countryside can yield good results, as Jürgenson proved. The date and time should be spoken into the microphone before each session, followed by an invitation to the voices to speak. Each recording session should be no longer than

approximately two minutes, as intense concentration is needed in listening to the playback of the voices.

Three basic recording methods are most likely to be of use. With the first, the tape recorder is simply switched to 'record'; then questions are asked aloud and details of them noted on paper.

With a second method, preliminary announcements are made through a microphone which is then unplugged and a radio attached to the recorder instead. The radio is tuned between frequencies, to a band of 'white noise', and the recording level is set mid-way between maximum and minimum.

A third method involves the use of a diode receiver, a small crystal set that is plugged into the microphone socket of a tape recorder.

Klaus Schreiber, retired German fire equipment inspector, right, claims to have gone one step beyond the recording of voices, and to have captured on television the image of his deceased daughter, Karin, above.

Under differing conditions and circumstances, a factory-clean tape, run through an ordinary tape-recording head in an otherwise silent environment, they found, will contain human voices speaking recognisable words when played back. The origin of these voices is apparently inexplicable in the light of present day science, and the voices themselves are objective in that they yield prints in the same way as normal voices, registering as visible oscillograph impulses on videotape recordings. The implications of these 'voices from nowhere' are enormous. Dr Bender himself is even reported to consider them of more importance to humanity than nuclear physics.

Other scientists, too, were to become fascinated by Jürgenson's odd discovery. Dr Konstantin

Raudive, former professor of psychology at the Universities of Uppsala and Riga, was living in Bad Krozingen, Germany, when he heard of the Jürgenson-Bender experiments in 1965. A former student of Carl Jung, Dr Raudive had been forced to flee from his native Latvia when it was invaded and annexed by the Soviet Union in 1945. Thereafter, he became well-known as a writer on experimental psychology.

Dr Raudive also began recording tests on the mysterious voices with conspicuous success; and between 1965 and his death in 1974, in partnership with physicist Dr Alex Schneider of St Gallen, Switzerland, and Theodor Rudolph, a specialist in high-frequency electronic engineering, he made over 100,000 tapes under stringent laboratory conditions. An exhaustive analysis of his work was published in Germany in the late 1960s, under the title *The Inaudible Made Audible*. This caught the attention of British publisher Colin Smythe, who subsequently brought out an English language edition, entitled *Breakthrough*.

Peter Bander, who wrote the preface to the book, later gave an account of how he first heard a strange voice on tape. This nicely illustrates what happens as a rule, and also points out the objective nature of the phenomenon. Colin Smythe had bought a new tape and had followed Dr Raudive's instructions on how to 'contact' the voices. A certain rhythm resembling a human voice had been recorded, but it was unintelligible to Smythe. Peter Bander played the relevant portion of tape over two or three times, and suddenly became aware of what the voice was saying. It was a woman's, and it said: *'Mach die Tur mal auf'* – German for *'Open the door'*. Bander immediately recognised the voice as that of his dead mother – he had been in the habit of conducting his correspondence with her by tape recordings for several years before she died. What is more, the comment was apt: his colleagues often chided him for shutting his office door.

Dr Konstantin Raudive is seen, right, with the 'goniometer', an instrument that was designed for him by Theodor Rudolph of Telefunken to record 'spirit' voices.

The Right Reverend Monsignor Stephen O'Connor, Vicar General and Principal Roman Catholic Chaplain to the Royal Navy at the time, listens to a voice recorded by Dr Raudive, below. The voice seemed to be that of a young naval officer who had committed suicide two years earlier.

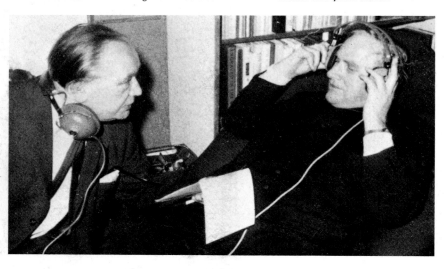

Startled by the voice, Bander asked two people who did not speak German to listen and write down what they heard phonetically. Their versions matched what he had heard exactly. Dr Bander was now convinced of the authenticity of the voices.

Since the publication of *Breakthrough* in 1971, serious research has begun in all parts of the world, and the interest of two very different bodies reflects the spiritual and temporal aspects of the voices. Even the Vatican has shown a great deal of 'off the record' awareness of the phenomena, and a number of distinguished Catholic priest-scientists have conducted experiments of their own. Pre-eminent among these researchers was the late Professor Gebhard Frei, an internationally recognised expert in the fields of depth psychology, parapsychology and anthropology. Dr Frei was the cousin of the late Pope Paul VI who, in 1969, decorated Friedrich Jürgenson with the Commander's Cross of the Order of St Gregory the Great, ostensibly for documentary film work about the Vatican. But, as Jürgenson told Peter Bander in August 1971, he had found 'a sympathetic ear for the voice phenomenon in the Vatican'.

The interest of the National Aeronautics and Space Administration (NASA) also came to light in the late 1960s when two American engineers from Cape Kennedy visited Dr Raudive at Bad Krozingen. The visitors examined Dr Raudive's experiments minutely and asked many 'unusually pertinent questions', as well as making helpful comments. They refused, unfortunately, to give the scientist any indication of what relevance the voice phenomena might have to America's space programme.

But as Dr Raudive reasoned, if he could achieve clear and regular results on his relatively simple equipment, how much more likely was it that the sophisticated recorders carried in spacecraft would pick up the voices? From whatever source they spring, Jürgenson's voices represent the start of a whole new field in the study of the paranormal.

Pope Paul VI, right, decorated Friedrich Jürgenson with the Commander's Cross of the Order of St Gregory the Great in 1969. The Catholic Church has never expressed an official opinion on the nature of his mysterious voices, but Jürgenson has said that he found 'a sympathetic ear' in the Vatican.